W9-BZV-864

813.52
NEW

c.1

New e   s on

L

DATE DUE

APR 2 5 200

813.52
NEW   New essays on

AUTHOR

TITLE   Light in August   c.1

DATE LOANED	BORROWER'S NAME	DATE RETURNED
APR 2 5 2005	Scott Goldstein Eloy	9154

HALL HIGH SCHOOL LIBRARY
WEST HARTFORD, CT 06117

DEMCO

★ The American Novel ★

GENERAL EDITOR

Emory Elliott, Princeton University

New Essays on
Light in August

Edited by

Michael Millgate

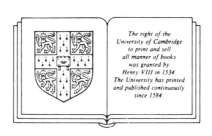

The right of the
University of *Cambridge*
to print and sell
all manner of books
was granted by
Henry VIII in 1534.
The University has printed
and published continuously
since 1584.

CAMBRIDGE UNIVERSITY PRESS

Cambridge

New York   New Rochelle   Melbourne   Sydney

HALL HIGH SCHOOL LIBRARY
WEST HARTFORD, CT 06117

Published by the Press Syndicate of the University of Cambridge
The Pitt Building, Trumpington Street, Cambridge CB2 1RP
32 East 57th Street, New York, NY 10022, USA
10 Stamford Road, Oakleigh, Melbourne 3166, Australia

© Cambridge University Press 1987

First published 1987

Printed in the United States of America

Library of Congress Cataloging-in-Publication Data
New essays on Light in August.
(The American novel)
Bibliography: p.
1. Faulkner, William, 1897–1962. Light in August.
I. Millgate, Michael. II. Series.
PS3511.A86L5754   1987   813'.52   86-33398

ISBN 0 521 30814 3 hard covers
ISBN 0 521 31332 5 paperback

British Library Cataloging-in-Publication data applied for.

813.52
NEW

c 1

Contents

Contents

Series Editor's Preface

In literary criticism the last twenty-five years have been particularly fruitful. Since the rise of the New Criticism in the 1950s, which focused attention of critics and readers upon the text itself – apart from history, biography, and society – there has emerged a wide variety of critical methods which have brought to literary works a rich diversity of perspectives: social, historical, political, psychological, economic, ideological, and philosophical. While attention to the text itself, as taught by the New Critics, remains at the core of contemporary interpretation, the widely shared assumption that works of art generate many different kinds of interpretation has opened up possibilities for new readings and new meanings.

Before this critical revolution, many American novels had come to be taken for granted by earlier generations of readers as having an established set of recognized interpretations. There was a sense among many students that the canon was established and that the larger thematic and interpretative issues had been decided. The task of the new reader was to examine the ways in which elements such as structure, style, and imagery contributed to each novel's acknowledged purpose. But recent criticism has brought these old assumptions into question and has thereby generated a wide variety of original, and often quite surprising, interpretations of the classics, as well as of rediscovered novels such as Kate Chopin's *The Awakening*, which has only recently entered the canon of works that scholars and critics study and that teachers assign their students.

The aim of The American Novel Series is to provide students of American literature and culture with introductory critical guides to

American novels now widely read and studied. Each volume is devoted to a single novel and begins with an introduction by the volume editor, a distinguished authority on the text. The introduction presents details of the novel's composition, publication history, and contemporary reception, as well as a survey of the major critical trends and readings from first publication to the present. This overview is followed by four or five original essays, specifically commissioned from senior scholars of established reputation and from outstanding younger critics. Each essay presents a distinct point of view, and together they constitute a forum of interpretative methods and of the best contemporary ideas on each text. It is our hope that these volumes will convey the vitality of current critical work in American literature, generate new insights and excitement for students of the American novel, and inspire new respect for and new perspectives upon these major literary texts.

Emory Elliott
Princeton University

1

Introduction

MICHAEL MILLGATE

W HEN his seventh novel, *Light in August*, was published in
October 1932, William Faulkner was just thirty-five years
old and at the peak of his creative powers. This is not to say that
his career, so shapely in its outlines, was ever marked by radical
shifts in the levels of his achievement: his first novel and his last
are both distinguished works, quite different from one another yet
alike in displaying the stamp of their author's genius. But there is
general agreement among Faulkner's readers and critics that the
years between 1928 and 1936 – years that saw the composition
and publication of *The Sound and the Fury, As I Lay Dying, Sanctuary, Light in August, Pylon,* and *Absalom, Absalom!,* as well as of
numerous short stories – constituted a period of extraordinarily
sustained creative activity, unmatched either in Faulkner's own
career or in that of any other American writer of the twentieth
century.

1

The exceptional intensity with which Faulkner worked at this time
perhaps had something to do with the relative slowness with
which he found his way into print – or, at least into public notice.
At a time when his near contemporaries F. Scott Fitzgerald, Ernest
Hemingway, and John Dos Passos were already established and,
indeed, famous writers – Fitzgerald's great success with *This Side of
Paradise* came in 1920, when he was only twenty-three years old –
Faulkner remained entirely unknown and almost entirely unpublished, hanging around the campus of the University of Mis-

sissippi, the French Quarter of New Orleans, or, more briefly, the fringes of the American expatriate world in Paris.

He had been born – "male and single at early age," as he once humorously declared[1] – in New Albany, in northern Mississippi, on September 25, 1897, but by the time he was five he had moved with his family to Oxford, the county town of Lafayette County, Mississippi, and the place he was later to use as the principal model for his fictional Jefferson, the focal point of Yoknapatawpha County. In Oxford he experienced the characteristic open-air upbringing of a Southern white youth of middle-class parents, and although he never finished high school he read omnivorously in his teens – the extent and depth of Faulkner's reading should never be underestimated – and began to write and draw. In 1918 he joined the British Royal Air Force and spent several months in Canada training to be a pilot, but the armistice of November 1918 came too soon for him even to get into the air, let alone to Europe. Back in Oxford he published a few poems, essays, and illustrations in campus newspapers and acted out a self-conscious, self-dramatizing role as a local poet; in 1924, encouraged and supported by his friend Phil Stone, an Oxford lawyer, he published with a "vanity" press a verse sequence in rhymed octosyllabic couplets entitled *The Marble Faun* – of which the few surviving copies have become extremely valuable collector's items. In the autumn of 1924, however, he met the novelist Sherwood Anderson, then at the height of his popularity, and his own first sustained attempts to write fiction seem to have belonged to the period of the six-month visit to New Orleans that began in January 1925 and ended with his departure in early July for a five-month tour of Europe.

Faulkner's first novel, *Soldiers' Pay,* written while he was in New Orleans and published in 1926, was an impressive achievement, ambitious as a piece of writing and strikingly effective in its treatment of the isolation and incomprehension encountered by soldiers returning from the World War I to a civilian world of which they seem no longer a part. A second novel, *Mosquitoes* (1927), was distinctly less successful, and in the autumn of 1927, after he had returned to Oxford and settled down to make a serious literary career for himself, Faulkner was badly shaken by his failure to find a publisher for the long and leisurely novel, drawing extensively on local observation and on his own family history, that he had confidently counted upon to make money, establish his reputation, and so provide a secure basis for his future career. *Flags in the Dust*, as it was originally called, did eventually appear in severely truncated form as *Sartoris* in January 1929,[2] establishing for the first time that world of Jefferson and Yoknapatawpha County that was to provide Faulkner with the setting for so many subsequent novels and stories. But in the meantime, according to his own account, Faulkner had written his guts into a new book, *The Sound and the Fury*, believing that he was fated to be an unpublished author and need therefore make no concessions to the conventionality and cautious commercialism of the literary marketplace. In a moving, and now famous, passage, written a few years later and never published in his own lifetime, Faulkner recalled:

> One day I seemed to shut a door between me and all publishers' addresses and book lists. I said to myself, Now I can write. Now I can make myself a vase like that which the old Roman kept at his bedside and wore the rim slowly away with kissing it. So I, who had never had a sister and was fated to lose my daughter in infancy, set out to make myself a beautiful and tragic little girl.[3]

The Sound and the Fury did find a publisher, however, despite the difficulties it posed and continues to pose for its readers, and from the moment of its appearance in October 1929 Faulkner never looked backward but moved always confidently forward to the exploration of new areas of experience, the development of new themes, and, above all, the confrontation of new technical challenges. Although his most strikingly obvious and distinctively "modern" experimentation appeared in *The Sound and the Fury* itself and, to a slightly lesser extent, in *As I Lay Dying*, the next of the novels to be published (in October 1930), Faulkner never repeated himself from a technical point of view, and in the long list, the impressively wide shelf, of his nineteen novels there are no two books that demonstrate precisely the same formal characteristics. Even the component volumes of the *Snopes* trilogy are quite different from one another in this respect, and the reader's entire relationship to the text of *The Reivers* (1962), Faulkner's final novel, is profoundly affected by its being placed within the framework implied by the two opening words: "GRANDFATHER SAID."[4]

Intervening between *As I Lay Dying* and *Light in August* in the sequence of Faulkner's publications was the controversial *Sanctuary*, brought out on February 9, 1931, but actually written and submitted to the publisher ahead of *As I Lay Dying*. Given the violence of the actions, including rape and murder, around which the narrative of *Sanctuary* is organized, it was perhaps hardly surprising that the reception of the novel, although predominantly favorable, should have been marked by expressions of revulsion and by the categorization of Faulkner, in an influential and by no means unappreciative review by Henry Seidel Canby, as a member of "the cruel school" of American fiction, a "prime example of American sadism."[5] Many aspects of the history of the composition of *Sanctuary* remain obscure, as do the reasons for the delay in its publication, but it is at least clear from Noel Polk's edition of *"Sanctuary": The Original Text* (1981) that the extensive revisions Faulkner made to the novel prior to publication were directed not toward diminishing its violence (which was, in fact, noticeably intensified) but rather toward simplifying its structure, cutting out the proliferating flashbacks of the earlier version and ordering the narrative into a more or less chronological sequence. In the process of making these changes, Faulkner abandoned his original opening, in which Horace Benbow, the central character, broods retrospectively upon events that have already occurred, in favor of the brilliantly conceived scene, formerly located in the second chapter, in which Benbow and the gangster, Popeye, stare across a spring at each other in absolute stillness for a period of two hours. It was a revision that not only provided a profoundly violent novel with a richly suggestive opening image of stasis and suspension but also worked with the existing (and essentially retained) ending of the book to constitute an overall ironic framework of such images.

Clearly, Faulkner's experience of restructuring *Sanctuary* was to have considerable implications for his strenuous endeavors to find an appropriate form for his next novel. *Light in August* was to look back to *Sanctuary* in its presentation of a number of parallel but only loosely connected lives, in its readiness to present violence with experiential directness and to set off episodes of violence against episodes of comedy, and in its adoption of some of the features of the contemporary American detective story – or at least, to adapt a phrase of André Malraux's, of the detective story as intruded upon by Greek tragedy. It might even be speculated that the long case history of Joe Christmas that occupies the center of *Light in August* was in some sense derived from the brief glimpse of Popeye's past life that Faulkner added to *Sanctuary* at the time of his final revision. Or that those suspended actions with which the published *Sanctuary* opens and closes had a significant bearing upon the use of Lena Grove at both the beginning and end of *Light in August*.

Whether or not the reviews of *Sanctuary* had any impact upon Faulkner's conception and execution of his next novel – whether, for example, they made any contribution to his apparent decision, at a fairly late stage, to present Joe Christmas in an altogether more sympathetic light – it is impossible to tell. What is clear, however, is that *Light in August*, like each of Faulkner's major works, needs to be seen both in its own terms, as a wholly autonomous work of art, and in terms of the moment in time and in Faulkner's career at which it was written. It has been suggested[6] that Faulkner in the early 1930s was working to a double agenda, seeking primarily to explore the fullest possible range of stylistic and structural techniques, to push excitedly toward the extreme limits of the novel form, and secondarily to give a denser substance and more complex integration to his fictional world of Yoknapatawpha. If this is true, then the case of *Light in August* takes on a peculiar interest. Although perceived as more conventional in technique than its immediate Faulknerian predecessors and successors, there can be no doubt that it makes heavy demands upon the reader in terms both of its structure and of its moral complexity. Widely regarded as a fable of the modern predicament, it is at the same time intensely of its regional place, profoundly concerned to develop further the sense of Jefferson's specificity and tangibility, to project it as an inescapably imaginable social fact. What is above all clear (as will be argued in my own essay later in this volume) is that Faulkner, always possessed of an imperious sense of his own responsibilities and capacities as an artist, embarked upon the composition of *Light in August* with an altogether exceptional determination to make it an unmistakably major work.

2

William Faulkner finished writing *Light in August* shortly after he first attained the status of a literary celebrity. He had received some good reviews from the very beginning of his career, *The Sound and the Fury* won him much respect in American literary circles, and in June 1930 the well-known English novelist Arnold Bennett hailed him as "the coming man," possessed of "inexhaustible invention, powerful imagination, a wondrous gift of characterization, a finished skill in dialogue," and capable of writing "like an angel."[7] But it was during a visit to New York in the autumn of 1931 that Faulkner seems first to have realized how greatly his fame had been enhanced by the mingled praise and outrage that had greeted the publication of *Sanctuary* the previous February. "I have created quite a sensation," he wrote home to his wife in Oxford, Mississippi, on November 13, 1931, adding that he had "learned with astonishment that I am now the most important figure in American letters. That is, I have the best future. . . . But I dont think it has gone to my head. Anyway, I am writing. Working on the novel, and on a short story which I think Cosmopolitan will pay me $1500.00 for."[8] Whatever short story this may have been, *Cosmopolitan* did not in fact buy it; but the novel was *Light in August*, and it was published ten months later, on October 6, 1932.

Although Faulkner's newly awakened sense of his literary reputation almost certainly contributed to the ambitiousness of the final scope and structure of *Light in August*, work on the novel had in fact begun some time before. The first page of the surviving manuscript (at the University of Virginia) is dated "Oxford, Mississippi/17 August, 1931," but it seems likely that a good deal of writing and a certain amount of reorganization had already taken place prior to that date. When talking about *Light in August* in later years, Faulkner said that its starting point in his imagination had been "Lena Grove, the idea of the young girl with nothing, pregnant, determined to find her sweetheart."[9] Other evidence suggests, however, that Faulkner may originally have conceived of the novel as beginning with the Reverend Gail Hightower sitting in his study, somewhat as he does at the beginning of chapter 3 of the novel as published: a surviving fragment of an early draft in Faulkner's hand at the University of Texas opens in this manner, and so, apparently, did the Virginia typescript at one stage in its evolution.[10] Faulkner's insistence on the primacy of the Lena Grove material — he said on another occasion that he had begun the book "knowing no more about it than a young woman, pregnant, walking along a strange country road"[11] — is further called into question by the fact that the Texas fragment, opening with Hightower, already carries the title "Light in August," even though Faulkner seems subsequently to have considered using the title "Dark House" that appears, struck through, on the first page of the Virginia manuscript.[12]

It seems entirely possible, however, that the novel in fact took shape from the coalescence of two (or more) narrative strands that were in the first place quite independently conceived. There are certainly elements in the opening chapter, including the introduction of Varner's store and of characters named Armstid and Winterbottom, that link the novel with the world of the Snopeses and their "poor white" sharecropping neighbors, a world that was to be fully explored only in the successive volumes of the *Snopes* trilogy — *The Hamlet* (1940), *The Town* (1957), and *The Mansion* (1959) — but that had already been established in *Sartoris* and in some of the many short stories Faulkner was writing and publishing in the early 1930s. And if the past-haunted figure of Hightower seems to have something in common with that of Dr. Gavin Blount in the unpublished short stories "The Big Shot," "Dull Tale," and "Rose of Lebanon,"[13] it is no less tempting to associate Joe Christmas with "Dry September," the short story about a lynching that Faulkner had published at the beginning of 1931.

Curiously enough, that abandoned title, "Dark House," later reappears as the title for an early draft of *Absalom, Absalom!* (1936), but here the link appears to consist of the part played in each novel (as in so many of Faulkner's works) by a decayed mansion, relic of a more prosperous past, that tends to be shunned by members of the local community as a house of ill omen. Given, however, the fact that in section VII of Tennyson's *In Memoriam*, Faulkner's apparent source, the "dark house" is a house of grief and mourning, it seems possible that Faulkner intended a hidden reference to the birth and death, just ten days later, of his first child in January 1931. The suggestion was once made that the book's final title glanced negatively at Lena Grove by its use of a country term for a pregnant cow's giving birth to its calf (hence becoming "light") in August; there seems little doubt, however, that Faulkner's allusion, anticipated in the Quentin section of *The Sound and the Fury* ("Some days in late August at home are like this, the air thin and eager like this, with something in it sad and nostalgic and familiar"),[14] and confirmed by the streaming rays of sunlight on the dust jacket and title page of the first edition of *Light in August* itself, was to a particular quality of light that he thought of as unique to his own part of the world.

Answering a questioner at the University of Virginia in 1957, he declared:

> [I]n August in Mississippi there's a few days somewhere about the middle of the month when suddenly there's a foretaste of fall, it's cool, there's a lambence, a luminous quality to the light, as though it came not from just today but from back in the old classic times. It might have fauns and satyrs and the gods and – from Greece, from Olympus in it somewhere. It lasts just for a day or two, then it's gone, but every year in August that occurs in my country, and that's all that title meant, it was just to me a pleasant evocative title because it reminded me of that time, of a luminosity older than our Christian civilization.[15]

Not surprisingly, perhaps, Faulkner went on to associate these ideas specifically with the "pagan quality" of Lena Grove – what he seems to have regarded, at least in retrospect, as her splendid amorality: "But as far as she was concerned, she didn't especially need any father for [her child], any more than the women that – on whom Jupiter begot children were anxious for a home and a father."[16] Presumably he also saw the title as emphasizing, in essentially the same terms, that element of moral fable, transcending the particularities of time and place, that runs not just through the Lena Grove strand of the novel but through the Hightower and Joe Christmas strands as well. And he must at some point have

8

realized that his title reflected not only his recurrent use of light/dark imagery but also those moments of illumination – of epiphany, of self-realization – experienced during that August of the novel's action by some of its central characters. So Byron Bunch falls in love with Lena at first sight; so Joe Christmas realizes that simple peace is what he has really been seeking all his life; so Hightower arrives at his final vision of human interdependence.

Because that date of August 17, 1931, on the first page of the *Light in August* manuscript may not necessarily represent the date on which Faulkner began work on the novel, it seems possible that it may memorialize instead a moment of special illumination or inspiration for the author himself – his own experience of "light in August." But if it was at this point that he first began to see the shape of the novel in its entirety, it was certainly some time later before that shape became fixed in its final, published form. Faulkner encountered during the writing of the novel many difficulties additional to those reflected in his changes of title and of narrative openings. The Virginia manuscript reveals frequent rearrangement of the ordering of chapters and much shifting around of smaller blocks of material. There is some evidence[17] that the opening Lena Grove chapter was at one point immediately followed by an introduction of Joe Christmas corresponding broadly to the present McEachern episode and ending with Joe's hitching a ride into Jefferson on the back of a truck and then acting with "white" aggressiveness toward two black youths he accidentally encounters. Inconclusive though this evidence is, it does point toward the interesting possibility that Faulkner may once have intended a juxtaposed contrast between Lena's and Joe's respective arrivals in Jefferson (one on a waggon, the other on a truck) substantially more direct and strident than the one established by the first two chapters of the published text. The same evidence also tends to support Regina Fadiman's plausible although unproven contention, in her detailed study of the novel's composition, that the flashback narration of Joe's previous life now occupying the center of the novel was assembled and placed in its present location only at a late stage in the book's evolution. *Sanctuary*, after all, had been extensively rewritten and reorganized even after it had been sent to the printer and set in type, and it was while he was writing *Light in August* itself that Faulkner told an interviewer that the plot of a novel was "anything that moves you enough to keep working on it. A story usually makes its own plot, works itself out as you go."[18]

Work on the novel proceeded throughout the final months of 1931 and the early weeks of 1932, although Faulkner's casualness about dating his letters makes it difficult to follow the precise rate and nature of his progress. A *New Yorker* interview published in late November 1931 refers to *Light in August* by that title and speaks of it as "about a quarter done"; the same interview supplies, beneath its slick surface, some indication of the intensity with which Faulkner was working at this period. "Ah write when the spirit moves me," he is reported as telling his interviewer, "and the spirit moves me every day."[19] He kept working at the book while he was in New York and elsewhere in November and early December of 1931 and again when he returned to Oxford, Mississippi, over Christmas and the New Year. And it was apparently at about this time that he was forced to do some rewriting of a portion of the present chapter 15 (332–4) as the result of losing one of the pages of his manuscript.[20]

In late January 1932 he told his agent, Ben Wasson, that he had not yet begun to type the novel for submission to a publisher, chiefly because it was "going too well" for him to want to risk interrupting the completion of the manuscript,[21] and in view of the fact that the manuscript bears on its final page the date "Oxford, Miss./19 Feb. 1932," it seems fairly clear that Faulkner did indeed finish it before doing much work on the typescript. That typescript (now divided between the universities of Virginia and Texas) shows that Faulkner continued to the end to make minor revisions and adjustments to his text; at the same time the absence of major discrepancies between the manuscript and the typescript suggests that he had no last-minute qualms about the structure of a novel that was later to be criticized for its lack of focus, organization, and narrative continuity. When, in the spring of 1932, he initiated an (unsuccessful) attempt to arrange for *Light in August* to be serialized, it was on condition that "no changes" be made in the text;[22] in September of that same year, after he had read the galley proofs, he reiterated to Wasson his sense of satisfaction with the book as it stood, declaring: "I dont see anything wrong with it."[23] Not surprisingly, the galleys (now at the University of Texas) show only minor corrections in Faulkner's hand, although he reacted with characteristic irritation (e.g., "O.K. as set, goddam it") to occasional suggestions by the publisher's reader for the improvement of his punctuation and prose style.[24]

Faulkner was in Hollywood for much of the spring, summer, and early fall of 1932, scriptwriting for Metro-Goldwyn-Mayer and responding to an inquiry as to the cinematic possibilities of *Light in August* with the suggestion that it would "make a good Mickey Mouse picture."[25] Although he had come back to Oxford on the occasion of his father's death in early August, he left again for California on October 3, just three days before *Light in August* was published in New York, and apparently did not see a copy of the first edition until he returned home toward the end of that same month. "The book looks fine," Faulkner then wrote to his publisher, although he was to declare on a later occasion that at the moment of his first seeing the book, his enthusiasm for writing was at such a low ebb that he "didn't even want to see what kind of jacket [Harrison] Smith had put on it."[26] Smith, whose faith in Faulkner's work and in his own judgment had been so largely responsible for the publication of *The Sound and the Fury*, had contracted for *Light in August* as an independent publisher: the salesman's dummy of the novel bore the one name, Harrison Smith, both on its spine and on its title page.[27] Some time between March and June 1932, however, Smith entered into a partnership with Robert Haas (a cofounder of the Book of the Month Club), and it was over the new Smith and Haas imprint that *Light in August* finally appeared on October 6, 1932, the dust jacket in question featuring those rays of sunlight to which reference has earlier been made. On the front flap was a blurb (clearly not Faulkner's own work) that made reference to the Reverend Hightowers and to a "mulatto" named *Lee* Christmas and characterized the novel as being "as luxuriant as a plant grown in the luxuriant soil of the delta of the Mississippi River" – as "less brutal" and "more human" than *Sanctuary* and "richer in the development of character and plot."

The new novel did reasonably though by no means spectacularly well. The first and second printings apparently ran to 8,500 and 2,500 copies, respectively; there were two more printings before the end of 1932, but a substantial number of copies (in sheets) of the fourth printing remained unsold when Random House took over Smith and Haas in 1936, and these were subsequently issued in a Random House binding but with the original imprint still on the title page. An English issue, very slightly bowdlerized (on line 25 of page 204 the English text has "taking" where the American reads "f——ing"), was brought out by Chatto & Windus in 1933 and a French translation, by Maurice Coindreau, appeared in 1935. After World War II, when Faulkner's status as a major figure of the modern movement first began to be recognized in North America (it had been visible for some time in continental Europe), *Light in August* was brought out by New Directions in an offset reissue of the first edition. The novel was reset by Random House for inclusion in the Modern Library in 1950, but in 1967 Random House abandoned this text in favor of a photographic reissue of the first edition, subsequently adopting this form for their Modern Library, Modern Library College, and Vintage Books issues as well. Most recently, in the fall of 1985, a new text of the novel, prepared by Noel Polk and based on Faulkner's typescript, has been presented by the Library of America in a volume entitled *Novels 1930–1935*.

3

In the years since Faulkner's reputation became fully and universally established *Light in August* has been consistently regarded as one of his greatest achievements – not, perhaps, as the very greatest, a position commonly reserved for those more obviously "brilliant" and modernist novels *The Sound and the Fury* and *Absalom, Absalom!*, but certainly as a major text, central to any evaluation or understanding of his career as a whole. And it was from the very first recognized as an important work. The standard generalizations about Faulkner's lack of recognition during the early stages of his career rarely survive the test of a close scrutiny of what was actually said at the time, and the reception of *Light in August*, at least in the principal American journals and newspapers, was in fact remarkably positive. Even Henry Seidel Canby, author of the "American sadism" review of *Sanctuary* the previous year,[28] made only minor reservations when praising *Light in August* in the *Saturday Review* of October 8, 1932:

> It is a novel of extraordinary force and insight, incredibly rich in character studies, intensely vivid, rising sometimes to poetry, and filled with that spirit of compassion which saves those which look at life too closely from hardness and despair. If the writing is sometimes as slovenly as at other times it is pointed and brilliant, if there are scenes too macabre, characters in whom fantasy transcends its just limits, and an obscurity, or rather, a turgidity in symbolism which is often annoying, this is merely to say that it is not a perfect work of art. . . . [Faulkner] needs self-discipline, and the discipline of study and reading, but he can be trusted to find his own way.[29]

In an important (because widely read) review in the *New York Times Book Review* of October 9, 1932, J. Donald Adams emphasized almost exactly the same points as Canby had done the day before:

> With this new novel, Mr. Faulkner has taken a tremendous stride forward. To say that "Light in August" is an astonishing performance is not to use the word lightly. That somewhat crude and altogether brutal power which thrust itself through his previous work is in this book disciplined to a greater effectiveness than one would have believed possible in so short a time.

Not only had Faulkner shown himself to be "a stylist of striking strength and beauty," Adams added, but he had allowed some of his characters "to act sometimes out of motives which are human in their decency. . . . He has learned justice and compassion."[30] What seems to emerge strongly, if not altogether explicitly, from both reviews is the extent to which the violence and (as they had seen it) sensationalism of *Sanctuary* had come to dominate their sense of Faulkner as a novelist, almost to the extent of blocking out appreciation or even memory of what he had done in such works as *The Sound and the Fury* and *As I Lay Dying*.

Several other critics wrote in broadly similar terms, mingling admiration of the novel overall with criticism – sometimes of a puzzled or irritated kind — of particular aspects of its structure, style, or characterization. James T. Farrell, himself a successful if very different novelist, opened his *New York Sun* review with an acknowledgment of Faulkner's "impressive stylistic competence" and "considerable virtuosity in construction and organization" and testified to the way in which the reader tended to be "swept along" almost unreflectingly by "the man's driving pen." At the same time, he objected strongly to the repetitiousness of Faulkner's style and to his indulgence in "tricks and mannerisms that have been termed 'modernistic,'"[31] notably that fondness for run-together words (as in "womansmell" or "childtrebling") an English critic was to castigate as "precioussilly."[32] In the second of two brief but favorable reviews he wrote of the novel, Herschel Brickell was similarly critical of Faulkner's indulgence in "trivial mannerisms, such as the coupling of words;[33] in the other, he observed that it would take more than a simple assertion of Faulkner's virtues to break down "the prejudice that exists against him among a good many people who will not even read him to find out whether or not they like him."[34]

Obviously, that prejudice had been largely provoked by the publicity given to the subject matter of *Sanctuary*, but some remarks by Evan Shipman in the *New Republic* of October 26, 1932, point to perceived sources of deterrence within *Light in August* itself:

> [*Light in August*] combines all the faults and some of the interesting qualities of his previous books. For instance the lack of unity in the handling of diverse themes is so marked as to seem a willful misleading of the reader. The extravagant style becomes ridiculous when, as often in four hundred pages, it is applied to the commonplace. It is hardly a supple medium. Much of the violence appears to be as formal a matter as in an Elizabethan "tragedy of blood."[35]

For Dorothy Van Doren, writing in the *Nation* of October 26, 1932, the trouble with *Light in August* lay in its return to the themes, actions, and situations of Faulkner's earlier fiction and in its tendency, as she saw it, to describe only what the characters did, not what they thought or felt. For Frederic Thompson, on the other hand, writing in the Catholic journal *Commonweal*, recognition of

the possibility of negative responses to Faulkner's work could co-
exist with a profound personal admiration:

> As for Faulkner's art, it is in its very extremity supreme among the
> works of modern writers of fiction in English prose. Its extremity,
> however, is no doubt self-isolating. That is, I have estimable friends
> who find Faulkner's method a thicket of words that stand impen-
> etrably between them and the pattern of his dream. For me, on the
> other hand, he has the supreme genius of being able to invest even
> humble people and little things with a sudden, strange imme-
> diateness; they suddenly stand out in naked objectivity in the pre-
> ternatural light and stillness of space-time. They have the thrilling
> drama of simple being that the average person is able to appreciate
> only at rare moments. And the sensitiveness and range of Faulk-
> ner's perceptions is amazing.[36]

It seems curious, in the light of a hindsighted realization of the
importance of Yoknapatawpha to Faulkner's sense of himself as an
artist, that the original reviewers of *Light in August* should have
placed so little stress on the specifically regional aspects of the
novel. They saw, indeed, that it was about the South, which most
of them (as northern city dwellers) automatically thought of as an
area of extreme social, political, and artistic backwardness, but
they showed little appreciation of the network of interrelationships and interreflections that Faulkner was already building up
among his novels and stories and that was to receive sharper definition with the inclusion of a map of his fictional county in the first
edition of *Absalom, Absalom!* less than four years later. Even
George Marion O'Donnell's review in the Memphis *Commercial
Appeal* – the major newspaper for the area of northern Mississippi
that Faulkner lived in and wrote about – did not go beyond the
recognition that *Light in August* was set in "Jefferson, Mississippi,
the locale of four of the six novels that have made him a major
writer." O'Donnell certainly showed, however, the keenest appreciation of the novel's texture and of the technical directions in
which Faulkner appeared to be moving. Although he noted the
"slight looseness" resulting from the extensive use of flashbacks,
he found the plot itself to be "luxuriant, teeming with a thousand
suggestions and implications and complications, but clear-cut and

lucid at last," and the narrative technique to be at once cumulative and synthetic:

> The author has employed third person, past tense, and present tense narration, the stream of consciousness, first person narration and conversation, blending the various methods that he has used separately in previous books into a whole that is admirably effective if not always smooth. This synchronization gives the impression that Faulkner is striving for a novel-form in which all modes will be blended into a perfect narrative. This perfection is not attained in *Light in August*, but it is approached.[37]

It seems unlikely, despite his lifelong anglophilia, that Faulkner paid any particular attention to the reviews of *Light in August* in the United Kingdom, where it appeared – ahead of *As I Lay Dying* and *These 13* – on January 12, 1933. In view, however, of the characteristic unresponsiveness of British readers to Faulkner's work in later years, it seems worth noting that the contemporary reviewers of *Light in August* were for the most part fully alert to its interest and distinction. It is true that some of the British notices were abruptly dismissive – Faulkner's new book, declared the *English Review*, "has all the repulsive qualities that his public has learned to love" – and that several critics, the novelist Compton Mackenzie among them, were impatient with what they saw as the excesses of Faulkner's style: "Page after page," wrote Cecil Roberts in the *Sphere*, "is filled with clumsy, ill-digested expressions, tortured sentences, and inappropriate adjectives."[38] It also seems possible that F. R. Leavis chose to review *Light in August* in the newly founded *Scrutiny* largely for the sake of attacking a writer already famous for his self-conscious modernism, arguing that in Faulkner the technique was not, as it should be, "the means of expressing firmly realized purpose, growing out of a personal sensibility," but simply "an expression of – or disguise for – an uncertainty about what he is trying to do."[39]

But it needs also to be said that the Mackenzie and Leavis reviews were by no means entirely hostile; that Richard Church described *Light in August* in the *Spectator* as "a great book," one that "burns throughout with a fierce indignation against cruelty, stupidity, and prejudice"; and that Richard Aldington called it a "passionately honest dissection of the dark places in the human soul."[40] For Jacob Isaacs the novel was

> a triumph of pre-envisaged management and inevitable construction. The interest of Mr. Faulkner's work does not lie in the mere story, though that is abundant and complex enough, but in the spatial deployment of his motive, and in the uncanny grip of time problems, and of verbal evocation and suggestion.[41]

And in *The Times Literary Supplement* an anonymous reviewer provided a powerful evocation of the novel's impact upon a reader encountering it for the first time:

> From threads of horror, hatred, lust, brutality, and obsession [Faulkner] weaves the intricate pattern of a tapestry dark indeed, yet rich and glowing with a thunderous threatening beauty. Life as he portrays it is terrible but vital; it *is* life, not merely existence; and the reader, even against his will, is compelled to participation by the sheer intensity of insight and expression, an almost rhapsodic assurance in intuition, a nearly tactile sensitiveness in the use of the colloquial prose.[42]

Some of the least perceptive and most hostile comments on Faulkner's work did indeed come from British critics and reviewers over the course of his career,[43] but the reception of *Light in August* in the United Kingdom was, if anything, more positive and perceptive than its reception in the United States itself – in part, perhaps, because the British reviewers did not need to confront so directly the bleakness of the novel's social and political implications.

4

Light in August was sufficiently established in the American literary imagination by August 1935 for it to become the subject of a parody – "Bright in August (A Faulknereality)" – in that month's issue of the *American Spectator*. That same year two American critics, James W. Linn and Houghton W. Taylor, offered a remarkably close analysis of the book's narrative techniques, including its persistent counterpointing of characters and stories, and in his introduction to the French translation of the novel, Maurice Edgar

Coindreau stressed the fundamental puritanism that he saw as providing Faulkner with both his subject matter and his angle of vision.[44] There is little doubt, however, that the general critical perception of *Light in August* — as of Faulkner's other early novels — was adversely affected during the late 1930s and the 1940s by the predominantly hostile reception accorded its successors, especially the more obviously difficult and overtly modernist *Pylon* (1935), *Absalom, Absalom!* (1936), and *The Wild Palms* (1939). At the same time, those critics who did write about Faulkner with intelligence and understanding tended to be fascinated precisely by the technical brilliance displayed in such texts and in *The Sound and the Fury* and *As I Lay Dying*. Thus in 1939 the poet-critic Conrad Aiken, commending Faulkner for his passionate interest in fictional form, could nonetheless describe *Light in August* as a failure, as lacking characters and stories sufficiently compelling to justify the sheer weight of its technical machinery: "Consequently what we see is an extraordinary power for form functioning relatively *in vacuo,* and existing only to sustain itself."[45] Warren Beck, on the other hand, writing on "William Faulkner's Style" in 1941, was by no means dismissive of the novel, but he paid only passing tribute to its "elegiac brooding" and to the "architectonics" of the three concluding chapters.[46] Joseph Warren Beach's *American Fiction 1920–1940,* a year later, similarly acknowledged the intricacy of the narrative patterns in the novel but made little attempt to analyze the way they functioned.

Beach was one of several early critics who made the error of describing Joe Christmas as a "mulatto," of assuming his "black blood" to be one of the narrative facts of the novel. By making this error central to his argument, another critic, Maxwell Geismar, was able to 1942 to conclude that *Light in August* reflected a twin hostile obsession with the Negro and the Female, the "twin Furies of the Faulknerian deep southern Waste Land," and that the sexual and social perversions ascribed to its characters — Joanna Burden and Joe Christmas in particular — were the expression of "a hatred of life so compelling with [Faulkner] that there almost seems to be an inability in the writer to reach maturity itself."[47] Confusion as to Joe's parentage occasionally recurs in more recent criticism, and Geismar's essay itself remained influential for many years – partly because the upsurge of interest in Faulkner's work in the 1950s, following the award of the Nobel Prize for Literature at the very beginning of that decade, ran for a time well ahead of the supply of close, intelligent critical discussions of individual texts.

Substantial criticism of *Light in August* had, however, begun in the late 1940s with Phyllis Hirshleifer's "As Whirlwinds in the South: An Analysis of *Light in August*" (*Perspective*, Summer 1949), an essay that provided its contemporaries with a far fuller and sounder reading of the novel than had previously been available, and with Richard Chase's more sophisticated but somewhat overstated symbolic interpretation, "The Stone and the Crucifixion: Faulkner's *Light in August*" (*Kenyon Review*, Autumn 1948). Of the several important studies that appeared during the course of the 1950s, most tended to focus either on the tragic and, as was often argued, the specifically modern aspects of the Joe Christmas story or on the moral and religious values that appeared to be central to the novel as a whole. The first of these categories was probably best represented by "Joe Christmas: The Hero in the Modern World," an essay by John L. Longley, Jr., that was subsequently included in his *The Tragic Mask: A Study of Faulkner's Heroes* (1963), the second by Ilse Dusoir Lind's "The Calvinistic Burden of *Light in August*" (*New England Quarterly*, September 1957), which saw Joe and Joanna as victims alike of their bleakly repressive and puritanical upbringings, and by C. Hugh Holman's "The Unity of Faulkner's *Light in August*" (*PMLA*, March 1958), which stressed – and, indeed, overstressed – the importance of the Christian symbolism in the novel as a source both of its positive values and of the minimal unity it was perceived as possessing.[48]

Olga W. Vickery's *The Novels of William Faulkner*, published in 1959, was the first, and one of the best, of a series of book-length general studies of Faulkner's work that marked the next stage (roughly coinciding with the 1960s) in the history of Faulkner criticism. Vickery emphasized the tension between the private selves of the major characters of *Light in August* and the public roles forced upon them by society. Collectively, she suggested, the town of Jefferson was "Southern, White, and Elect, qualities which have meaning only within a context which recognizes something or someone as Northern or Black or Damned," and Joanna Burden, Joe Christmas, and Hightower were scapegoat figures almost ritually sacrificed as representing, "in fact or popular conviction, those qualities which must be rejected if Jefferson is to maintain its self-defined character."[49] The effective, if somewhat too schematic, argument of the essay as a whole was in some respects challenged, in others reinforced, by the position taken by Cleanth Brooks in the *Light in August* chapter of his magisterial *William Faulkner: The Yoknapatawpha Country* (1963). For Brooks the entire structure and meaning of the novel fell into place in terms of the relationship between the principal characters ("pariahs, defiant exiles, withdrawn quietists, or simply strangers") and the community, seen as the embodiment of stable, traditional values and invoked in strongly positive terms as "the powerful though invisible force that quietly exerts itself in so much of Faulkner's work," as "the circumambient atmosphere, the essential ether" of his fiction.[50] Persuasive and influential as Brooks's discussion has proved, it does have the weakness of understating the many negative aspects of Jefferson society – notably its racial intolerance and propensity for violence – and, as Thomas L. McHaney has argued, of exaggerating the specificity with which that society and its values are in fact created in the novel. McHaney, although acknowledging the function of the community as a general, often contrastive, background to the fates of individual characters, also insists that to overemphasize that function is to deflect attention from Faulkner's primary concern with the characters themselves.[51]

Michael Millgate's chapter in another of the general books of the 1960s, *The Achievement of William Faulkner* (1966), was important for its early discussion of the genesis of the novel, its exploration of the interrelationships among the major characters and the narratives associated with them, and its speculations about Faulkner's invocation of various mythic frameworks – a topic also taken up by Walter Brylowski in *Faulkner's Olympian Laugh: Myth in the Novels* (1968). By the 1970s, however, the need was increasingly for more extended and detailed treatments of the novel, and three works produced early in the decade made significant contributions in this respect. François Pitavy's *Faulkner's "Light in August"*, first published in France in 1970, was revised and enlarged for its appearance in an English translation in 1973; it contained an admirably wide-ranging study of the novel's origins, reception, techniques, themes, characterization, and style. Particularly valuable in many respects were its observations on Faulkner's use of landscape in the novel and on the distinction of his writing, seen by Pitavy as characterized by its remarkable precision, intensity, and rhythmic control, and by its dense, striking, and often recurrent imagery. The "grandeur" of *Light in August*, as Pitavy puts it, depends in large measure upon "the mastery of its style, a style in which a poetic sense of rhythm and sound, a powerful imagination and a steady control of technique remain firmly harnessed to the author's purposes."[52] Still more comprehensive in some respects, especially in terms of its chapter-by-chapter analysis of the novel and its coverage of textual matters, was Carl Ficken's 1972 University of South Carolina dissertation, "A Textual and Critical Study of William Faulkner's *Light in August*."[53] Finally, in 1975, Regina K. Fadiman published *Faulkner's "Light in August": A Description and Interpretation of the Revisions*, a book whose importance has already been acknowledged in this introduction but that needs to be read in conjunction with the studies by Ficken and Pitavy — and with the latter's review in the Summer 1976 issue of the *Mississippi Quarterly*.

Some sense of the trends of *Light in August* criticism in recent years can be conveniently gained from *William Faulkner's "Light in August": A Critical Casebook*, edited by Pitavy and published in 1982. In addition to a number of earlier essays — including the still valuable "Faulkner's Joe Christmas: Character through Voice" by Sister Kristin Morrison, IHM, first published in 1961 — it contains a comprehensive and up-to-date annotated bibliography, revised versions of two sections (on voice and on style) from Pitavy's book on the novel, a useful new introduction by him, and four pieces from the late 1970s and early 1980s. Two of these, one an extract from Donald M. Kartiganer's *The Fragile Thread: The Meaning of Form in Faulkner's Novels* (1979), the other a reprinting of Carole Anne Taylor's "*Light in August*: The Epistemology of Tragic Paradox" (*Texas Studies in Literature and Language*, Spring 1980), explore questions relating to the language of the novel and the sense of identity of Joe Christmas and other major characters. A third essay, by Lee Clinton Jenkins, makes an early contribution to a recently renewed interest in the racial aspects of *Light in August* that has thus far been best served by Thadious M. Davis in *Faulkner's "Negro": Art and the Southern Context* (1983), and the fourth, by Stephen Meats, sorts out the complexities of the novel's chronology — an aspect independently explored by Harold Hungerford in the April 1983 issue of *American Literature.*

These are not, of course, the only areas of interest to critics of *Light in August* in the latter half of the 1980s — although it has to be said that the novel has received considerably less attention of late than such texts as *The Sound and the Fury, As I Lay Dying,* and *Absalom, Absalom!.* Other recent studies have dealt with its structure, its ending, and its biographical implications; Michel Gresset has a sensitive chapter focusing on Lena Grove in his *Faulkner ou la fascination* (1982); another distinguished French critic, André Bleikasten, has written briefly but trenchantly on the psychology of the novel in his essay entitled "Fathers in Faulkner."[54] Bleikasten's very impressive *Parcours de Faulkner* (1982) remains, like Gresset's book, unavailable in English as yet, but its extensive treatment of *Light in August* has been drawn upon by the author for his essay in the present volume.

5

Bleikasten's wide-ranging essay is preceded here by two essays that deal more specifically with Faulkner's ambitions for the novel and with the reader's experience in approaching it for the first time. The editor's own contribution is largely concerned to pick up and develop some of the central themes and topics already touched upon in this introduction. It seeks, in particular, to show that *Light in August* was the spectacularly successful outcome of a determination on Faulkner's part to establish his career, once and for all, on a secure and unchallengeable basis. Known already as, on the one hand, the brilliant experimentalist of *The Sound and the Fury* and, on the other, as the tough and even brutal realist of *Sanctuary,* he seems to have sought to reconcile those two aspects of his reputation in terms of a work that would place him firmly in the ranks of major American writers and in the mainstream of American fiction. But the apparent modification of the post-Joycean techniques that had been so evident in *The Sound and the Fury* and *As I Lay Dying* did not imply any diminution of the complexity of the new novel. *Light in August* made heavy demands upon its readers in moral and intellectual terms because its central characters (apart from the pervasively contrastive figure of Lena Grove) led such dark and troubled lives and were presented from so many and such different points of view. It remained technically difficult because of the jaggedness of its structure and the refusal of its parallel plot lines to merge into moments of final, comprehensive resolution. And the fact that Faulkner, in a book written with such stylistic deliberation, should make so little attempt to smooth off the roughness of its narrative edges constituted a clear indication that there existed no single key capable of closing the lock upon its always outward-thrusting openness.

Martin Kreiswirth's essay, the second in the volume, deals in much greater detail with the narrative progression of the novel and with the ways in which the reader's expectations are continually being frustrated or deflected in favor of new plot developments, often involving newly introduced characters. Plots ostensibly comic may suddenly take an unexpected twist in the direction of tragedy. The forward linear movement characteristic of plots is repeatedly countered by the intrusion of other plot lines that retroactively seek to expose the secrets or as-yet unknowns of the past. The separate plots organized around the principal characters maintain throughout a kind of structural dialogue that is always active and never, even in the closing chapters, definitively resolved, while the fundamental self-division within such a figure as Joe Christmas is at once reflected in and sustained by the split and persistently blocked character of the narratives associated with him. The great strength and interest of Kreiswirth's contribution lies in the closeness with which it explores central elements in the novel's structure and reconstructs the experience of the reader as he or she moves into and through the text.

Bleikasten's title, *"Light in August:* The Closed Society and Its Subjects,"* provides an excellent indication of his central concern with the ways in which the novel's major and minor characters are alike affected by and reflective of their society's established values and assumptions. Taking a generally negative view of Cleanth Brooks's conception of the "community," Bleikasten insists that the pervasive presence of racist and sexist attitudes is responsible for the profound psychological damage suffered by so many of the characters and for the social ostracism and even death by violence to which they are too often driven. He then moves beyond such observations to a broader consideration of the repressive nature of the Puritan ideology that both endorses and underlies the entire value system of the world presented in *Light in August* and goes on to argue that a society grounded in such clear-cut divisions between white and black, male and female, election and damnation must necessarily compel absolute and unambiguous conformity from its members and from those outsiders who venture within its boundaries. It is this coherent explication of the interdependent functioning of racial, sexual, and religious obsessions within the novel that constitutes perhaps the single most valuable aspect of an altogether important essay.

Bleikasten does not, even so, exhaust the issue of sexism in the world of *Light in August* and in the imagination of William Faulkner, and several additional aspects of the topic are examined by Judith Wittenberg in the fourth essay in this volume. Well aware of the fact that Faulkner has sometimes been discussed as a misogynistic writer – most powerfully, perhaps, by Albert J. Guerard in *The Triumph of the Novel: Dickens, Dostoevsky, Faulkner* (1976) – Wittenberg offers a systematic and scrupulous account of the novel's female characters that nicely balances an appreciation of the roles they are forced to play within the male-dominated world of Jefferson with a sense of the emotional impact likely to be created in the reader by exposure to their generally complex psychological conditions and their often disastrous fates. Discussion of the women characters in *Light in August* has tended to focus almost exclusively on Lena Grove and Joanna Burden. By taking into account the lives and personalities of minor as well as major figures, Wittenberg provides a striking demonstration of the richness and variety of Faulkner's creativity within this particular text, as well as of his profound understanding of the practical and emotional consequences likely to follow for individual women not

24

simply from the basic fact of living within a society such as Jefferson's but also from the particularities of their economic situation, marital status, family upbringing, and genetic inheritance.

The final essay, by Alexander Welsh, moves in directions quite distinct from those pursued by any of its predecessors. Taking as its starting point a distinction drawn by Erik H. Erikson between two kinds of heroism, the one active and combative, the other passive and self-sacrificial, it considers the appropriateness of these categories to the characterization of such figures as Joe Christmas and Gail Hightower and, at a further range, to the opposition between human prevailing and enduring that Faulkner appeared to posit in his Nobel Prize address of 1950. In so doing, Welsh moves widely and wisely over a range of related issues within *Light in August* itself – offering in the process an account of Faulkner's attitudes toward women that is closer to Guerard's than to Wittenberg's – and implicitly invites the reader to withdraw a little from intensive engagement with the actual text of the novel and contemplate Faulkner and his work within larger and broader contexts, in terms of the historical development both of literature and of thought. As representing the cooler, less committed perspective of a distinguished critic who is by no means a "professional" Faulknerian, the essay has its proper and necessary place within a collection such as this – and if that place is, in practice, the final one, that is only because Welsh has most to offer to the reader who already feels secure in his or her own grasp of *Light in August* and of the terms in which that novel has been and is being discussed and evaluated by scholars and critics working within the Faulkner field.

NOTES

1. *Forum* 83 (April 1930):lvi. The principal source for biographical information about Faulkner is Joseph Blotner's *Faulkner: A Biography* (New York: Random House), first published in two volumes in 1974; a revised one-volume version appeared in 1984.
2. It was published in full only in 1973, eleven years after Faulkner's death.

3. "An Introduction for *The Sound and the Fury*," ed. James B. Meriwether, *Southern Review* n.s. 8 (Autumn 1972):710.

4. *The Reivers* (New York: Random House, 1962), p. 3.

5. "The School of Cruelty," *Saturday Review of Literature*, March 21, 1931; reprinted in John Bassett, ed., *William Faulkner: The Critical Heritage* (London: Routledge & Kegan Paul, 1975), p. 109.

6. See Michael Millgate, "William Faulkner: The Shape of a Career," in Doreen Fowler and Ann J. Abadie, eds., *New Directions in Faulkner Studies: Faulkner and Yoknapatawpha, 1983* (Jackson: University Press of Mississippi, 1984), pp. 18–36.

7. Quoted in Bassett, ed., *Critical Heritage*, pp. 61–2.

8. *Selected Letters of William Faulkner*, ed. Joseph Blotner (New York: Random House, 1977), p. 53.

9. *Faulkner in the University: Class Conferences at the University of Virginia 1957–1958*, ed. Frederick L. Gwynn and Joseph L. Blotner (Charlottesville: University of Virginia Press, 1959), p. 74.

10. Regina K. Fadiman, *Faulkner's "Light in August": A Description and Interpretation of the Revisions* (Charlottesville: University Press of Virginia, 1975), pp. 33–4.

11. "An Introduction for *The Sound and the Fury*," 709.

12. Carl F. W. Ficken suggests in "A Textual and Critical Study of William Faulkner's *Light in August*" (Ph.D. diss., University of South Carolina, 1972) that the Texas fragment could have been the intended opening of a short story (p. 272); he also suggests that another fragment at Texas, dealing with Joe Christmas's giving himself up, could also have been a trial opening for a story or novel (p. 275).

13. See Michael Millgate, *The Achievement of William Faulkner* (London: Constable, 1966), 130–1; all three stories, the last under the title "A Return," are now available in *Uncollected Stories of William Faulkner*, ed. Joseph Blotner (New York: Random House, 1975).

14. William Faulkner, *The Sound and the Fury* (New York: Jonathan Cape and Harrison Smith, 1929), p. 153.

15. Gwynn and Blotner, eds., *Faulkner in the University*, p. 199.

16. Ibid.

17. At the University of Texas are some manuscript sheets that represent attempts made by Milton Abernethy, a literary friend of Faulkner's, to decipher some early sections of the manuscript of *Light in August* as it stood in late October 1931. Pathetically inadequate as transcriptions, these pages do nonetheless appear to preserve some useful information about one stage in the novel's composition.

18. *Lion in the Garden: Interviews with William Faulkner 1926–1962,* ed. James B. Meriwether and Michael Millgate (New York: Random House, 1968), p. 17.

19. Ibid., pp. 23, 24.

20. See William Faulkner, *"Light in August:* A Manuscript Fragment," ed. Deborah Thompson, *Mississippi Quarterly* 32 (Summer 1979): 477–80; Carl Petersen, *On the Track of the Dixie Limited: Further Notes of a Faulkner Collector* (LaGrange, Illinois: Colophon Book Shop, 1979), p. 21; and Blotner, ed., *Selected Letters,* p. 59.

21. Blotner, ed., *Selected Letters,* p. 59.

22. Ibid., p. 62; see also p. 61.

23. Ibid., p. 66.

24. Blotner, *Faulkner: A Biography* (1974), p. 784.

25. Blotner, ed., *Selected Letters,* p. 65.

26. Ibid., p. 66; "An Introduction for *The Sound and the Fury,"* 710.

27. See Carl Ficken, "The Opening Scene of Faulkner's *Light in August," Proof: The Yearbook of American Bibliographical and Textual Studies* 2 (1972):177; as Ficken points out, the dummy appears to preserve a version of the opening that Faulkner later revised.

28. Bassett, ed., *Critical Heritage,* p. 109. This anthology, with its introduction, provides a useful but necessarily selective overview of the reception of Faulkner's work in the United States and Britain; see also O. B. Emerson, *Faulkner's Early Literary Reception in America* (Ann Arbor, Mich.: UMI Research Press, 1984).

29. "The Grain of Life," *Saturday Review of Literature,* October 8, 1932, p. 156.

30. "Mr. Faulkner's Astonishing Novel," *New York Times Book Review,* October 9, 1932, p. 6.

31. Bassett, ed., *Critical Heritage,* pp. 136–7.

32. James Agate, "Some New Books," *Daily Express,* February 9, 1933, p. 8.

33. "The Fruits of Diversity," *Virginia Quarterly Review* 9 (January 1933):117.

34. "The Literary Landscape," *North American Review* 234 (December 1932):571.

35. *New Republic,* October 26, 1932, p. 300.

36. "American Decadence," *Commonweal,* November 30, 1932, p. 139.

37. Bassett, ed., *Critical Heritage,* p. 139.

38. *English Review* 56 (February 1933):226; *Sphere,* February 11, 1933, p. 200; Mackenzie's review appeared in the *Daily Mail,* February 9, 1933, and is quoted in Bassett, ed., *Critical Heritage,* pp. 142–3.

39. Bassett, ed., *Critical Heritage*, pp. 143–4.
40. *Spectator,* February 17, 1933, p. 226; Aldington's *Evening Standard* review of February 2, 1933, is quoted in Bassett, ed., *Critical Heritage*, pp. 140–1.
41. *Annual Register,* 1933, Part II, p. 37.
42. *The Times Literary Supplement,* February 16, 1933, p. 106.
43. On the general question of Faulkner's reception in the United Kingdom, see Gordon Price-Stephens, "The British Reception of William Faulkner 1919–1962," *Mississippi Quarterly* 18 (Summer 1965):119–200; Cleanth Brooks, "The British Reception of Faulkner's Work," in W. T. Zyla and W. M. Aycock, eds., *Prevailing Verities and World Literature* (Lubbock: Texas Tech University, 1973), pp. 41–55; and especially Mick Gidley, "Faulkner and the British: Episodes in a Literary Relationship," in Doreen Fowler and Ann J. Abadie, eds., *Faulkner: International Perspectives* (Jackson: University Press of Mississippi, 1984), pp. 74–96.
44. Linn and Taylor, *A Foreword to Fiction* (New York: Appleton-Century, 1935); Coindreau's introduction is included, in translation, in his *The Time of William Faulkner: A French View of Modern American Fiction,* ed. George McMillan Reeves (Columbia: University of South Carolina Press, 1971).
45. "William Faulkner: The Novel as Form," *Atlantic Monthly,* November 1939, quoted in Bassett, ed., *Critical Heritage,* p. 248.
46. Beck, "William Faulkner's Style," in *American Prefaces* (Spring 1941); quoted in Linda Welshimer Wagner, ed., *William Faulkner: Four Decades of Criticism* (East Lansing: Michigan State University Press, 1973), pp. 144, 141.
47. *Writers in Crisis: The American Novel Between Two Wars* (Boston: Houghton Mifflin, 1942), pp. 169, 168.
48. For differing contemporary perspectives on the mythic elements, see Beach Langston, "The Meaning of Lena Grove and Gail Hightower in *Light in August*" (*Boston University Studies in English,* Spring 1961), and especially Robert M. Slabey, "Myth and Ritual in *Light in August*" (*Texas Studies in Literature and Language,* Autumn 1960).
49. *The Novels of William Faulkner* (Baton Rouge: Louisiana State University Press, 1959), pp. 67, 68; a revised edition appeared in 1964.
50. *William Faulkner: The Yoknapatawpha Country* (New Haven, Conn.: Yale University Press, 1963), pp. 53, 52; see also his introduction to the 1967 Modern Library paperback reissue of *Light in August* and his discussion of the novel's chronology in *William Faulkner: Toward Yok-*

napatawpha and Beyond (New Haven, Conn.: Yale University Press, 1978), pp. 426–9.

51. "Brooks on Faulkner: The End of the Long View," *Review* 1 (1979): 29–45.

52. *Faulkner's "Light in August"*, trans. Gillian E. Cook (Bloomington: Indiana University Press, 1973), p. 150.

53. It remains unpublished but is available on microfilm from University Microfilms International, 300 N. Zeeb Road, Ann Arbor, MI 48106.

54. In Robert Con Davis, ed., *The Fictional Father: Lacanian Readings of the Text* (Amherst: University of Massachusetts Press, 1981).

2

"A Novel: Not an Anecdote": Faulkner's *Light in August*

MICHAEL MILLGATE

ALTHOUGH it is one of the most frequently taught and discussed of all of Faulkner's works, *Light in August* nevertheless remains one of the most troubling to many readers, one of the hardest to bring into either intellectual or aesthetic focus, hence one of the least understood. Clearly, these difficulties do not spring from any failure on the author's part but rather from the fact that the novel was from its inception an extremely ambitious work in which he made an unusually heavy and self-conscious creative investment, many of the problematic elements within the book being precisely those that relate most intimately to the sheer scope and scale of Faulkner's aspirations for it.

Faulkner's sense of achievement upon the completion of *Light in August* emerges strongly from the letter he wrote to his friend and agent, Ben Wasson, in the early autumn of 1932, immediately after reading the book through in galley proof: "I dont see anything wrong with it. I want it to stand as it is. This one is a novel: not an anecdote; that's why it seems topheavy, perhaps."[1] The distinct note of defensiveness in Faulkner's denial of "anything wrong with" the book and his insistence on its standing "as it is" perhaps suggest that he had encountered some criticism and resistance either from Wasson himself or, more probably, from the publisher, Harrison Smith – the man who had been adventurous enough to publish *The Sound and the Fury* just three years before and who remained sufficiently devoted to Faulkner's work to bring out his volume of poems, *A Green Bough,* in April 1933. *Light in August* was, after all, to be the longest of all of Faulkner's novels, and if it seemed on the surface a less "difficult" work than some of its predecessors, it remained loose in organization and often violent in content. Even someone who admired Faulkner's work as much as Harrison Smith might well have been disconcerted by the shift from the powerful and even vertiginous centripetal tendencies of novels like *The Sound and the Fury* and *As I Lay Dying* to the persistently and even, it must have seemed, wilfully centrifugal movement of *Light in August*. Faulkner, however, was perfectly clear and confident as to what he had done, though perhaps acknowledging, in that phrase about its seeming "topheavy," that he had loaded − and run the risk of overloading − the novel with an extraordinary number and range of characters and of main and subsidiary narrative sequences.

His reasons for taking such a risk and working on such a scale are hinted at in the assertion "This one is a novel: not an anecdote." At one level, of course, it is possible to interpret this as meaning that *Light in August*, the completed novel, was an altogether more substantial achievement than the relatively brief and limited narrative conception from which it sprang. Faulkner had used the word "anecdote" earlier in 1932 in referring to his surprised discovery, after completing the writing of *The Sound and the Fury*, that he had incorporated within the novel what he called "the anecdote of the girl who ran away with the man from the traveling show,"[2] and it is curious, if perhaps not very significant, that there should be certain similarities between Miss Quentin's situation in the earlier novel and the situations of both Lena Grove and Milly Hines in *Light in August*. If, however, Faulkner did have any specific narrative source in mind, it seems much more likely to have been the episode, remembered from his own childhood, of the lynching of Nelse Patton, a black man from the Oxford, Mississippi, area who had murdered a white woman by cutting her throat so effectively with a razor as almost to decapitate her.[3] Or he may have been thinking of that episode as mediated by his short story about a lynching, "Dry September," first published in 1931, in which the juxtaposition of sharply contrasted scenes creates for the reader much the same kind of enforced revaluation of initial assumptions as is compelled in *Light in August* by postponing any internal view of Joe Christmas until after his social hostility has become firmly established. In the story Miss Minnie Cooper seems plausible until the reader is given a glimpse of her psychological condition; similarly Joe Christmas appears simply hateful until the reader begins to understand what lies behind and beneath his public self. The links between the two texts are, indeed, specifically emphasized by the fact that Captain McLendon, who leads the lynching party in "Dry September," is also referred to in the novel.[4]

Of course, when Faulkner said "This one is a novel," he may simply have been seeking to distinguish *Light in August* from the short stories to which he had been devoting much of his professional attention since the publication of *Sanctuary*. His main task immediately preceding the commencement of work on *Light in August* was in fact the pulling together of the collection of short stories that he entitled *These 13* and dedicated to his wife and to their dead daughter – a task and dedication that perhaps played their part in enabling him to work through his grief and put it to some extent behind him. But it seems most likely, after all, that Faulkner's "This one" meant primarily "this novel," as distinct from other novels, and carried with it the implication that at least some of the volumes written and published prior to *Light in August* were, in his view, not novels but anecdotes. It is difficult to think of a book such as *The Sound and the Fury* in such limiting terms, except insofar as the entire novel can be seen as an elaboration of the original story of the Compson children on the night of their grandmother's funeral. But *As I Lay Dying*, which seems to have had a specifically anecdotal source,[5] remains focused on a fundamentally simple sequence of narrative actions, and *Sanctuary*, although less tightly structured, focuses throughout upon the causes and consequences of Temple's rape, itself suggested (according to Carvel Collins) by an anecdote told to Faulkner in a Memphis bar.[6]

What, then, was to be different about *Light in August*? Although the novel apparently grew from something even less substantial than an anecdote, the vision of Lena Grove walking along a country road, it was allowed and encouraged to expand and develop on a scale unprecedented even in *Flags in the Dust*, that loose, baggy monster of a novel that during Faulkner's lifetime achieved publication only in the drastically shortened form of *Sartoris*. As already suggested in the introduction to the present volume, Faulkner sought in writing *Light in August* to profit from the experience gained during his revision of *Sanctuary*, but he conceived of the new novel on a far grander scale. It was not simply that he created more than sixty named characters in the new book – as well as several unnamed characters and a whole community of undifferentiated Jeffersonians – but that he did not hesitate to develop their stories at extraordinary length, to introduce them suddenly, to dismiss them with equal suddenness and absoluteness, or to keep them separate from one another, as if within quite independent narratives.

Faulkner exercised a wholly new degree of structural freedom in composing *Light in August*, allowing each narrative sequence to expand according to its own inherent logic, introducing each new sequence and each new character at precisely the point required in order to throw the maximum illumination upon some nodal point in the action – usually one of those moments of arrested time that he sought so persistently to explore and understand in terms of the full multiplicity and complexity of all of their implications in the present and all of their antecedents from the past. So the extended flashback over the career of Joe Christmas is poised upon the moment immediately preceding his final confrontation with Joanna Burden. So, at a late point in the novel, Gavin Stevens and Percy Grimm are abruptly introduced purely for the sake of their bearing upon the climactic moment of Christmas's own death: "Gavin Stevens though had a different theory," it is suddenly announced in the second paragraph of chapter 19 (419), although no such character has previously been mentioned. And the moment Stevens's account is concluded, the other figure steps forward: "In the town on that day lived a young man named Percy Grimm" (425). Even more remarkable in some respects are the unheralded excursions into the family backgrounds of Joanna Burden on the one hand and Gail Hightower on the other.

Fundamental to narrative expansion of this kind and scale was Faulkner's creation of space within which to work, his preparation of a canvas for the deployment of his numerous characters and quasi-independent narratives, the manipulation of his multiple

34

time shifts. The opening chapter moves back and forth with extraordinary rapidity between different times, different tenses, and different levels not simply of Lena's consciousness but of the narrative presentation of that consciousness. Immediately following the first direct-speech expression of Lena's thoughts ("Lena thinks, 'I have come from Alabama: a fur piece. All the way from Alabama a-walking. A fur piece.'"), Faulkner shifts, somewhat as in *As I Lay Dying*, to a convention that allows him to elaborate Lena's thoughts without restricting himself to Lena's own linguistic resources:

> Thinking *although I have not been quite a month on the road I am already in Mississippi, further from home than I have ever been before. I am now further from Doane's Mill than I have been since I was twelve years old* (p. 1)

Characteristically the passage is left without a final period, allowing the unconcluded − for Lena, the unconcludable − thought process to remain suspended, like so much else in this opening chapter. Equally characteristically, the implicit glance forward constituted by the unfinished sentence is immediately countered by an explanatory flashback, blocking in all that the reader needs to be told of a past that those who encounter Lena within the novel are able to reconstruct at a glance.

And so that opening chapter continues, alternating between internal and external views of characters and moving swiftly over the events of lifetimes − summarizing Lena's past life in a paragraph or two, disposing of her parents in a couple of sentences, and covering the birth, life, and death of the hamlet of Doane's Mill in just a sentence or two more. The brief course of Lena's seduction by Lucas Burch, alias Joe Brown, is told with a crisp inevitability that gives it almost the character of a medieval fable, and her subsequent travels on the road to Jefferson are evoked in terms of the timeless permanence of myth and of art itself: "like something moving forever and without progress across an urn" (5). This sense of suspension, endorsed by the deliberate allusion to Keats's "Ode on a Grecian Urn," is further confirmed by the next paragraph's insistence on the infinite slowness of Armstid's wagon, the sounds of its almost imperceptible progress "carrying for a half mile across the hot still pinewiney silence of the August afternoon" (5).

The impression of stasis, of absolute stillness, imposed by the oppressive heat is reinforced by the expansiveness of the setting itself: "The wagon moves slowly, steadily, as if here within the sunny loneliness of the enormous land it were outside of, beyond all time and all haste" (24). The opening chapter establishes, in fact, the prospect and promise of almost unlimited time and space – a suspension permissive of constant slippage between tenses, of the withholding of actions, and of the radical exploration and manipulation of time itself. That openness is, of course, exploited with great virtuosity throughout the remainder of the novel – especially in the extraordinary resourcefulness of its style and the subtlety of its shifts in time and narrative perspective – but even before the end of the first chapter it becomes possible for Lena's relationship with the Armstids, husband and wife, to be developed with a leisureliness and particularity that are altogether less suggestive of the kind of novel that is to follow than of some pastoral fiction along the lines of Hardy's *Tess of the d'Urbervilles* or even of Faulkner's *The Hamlet*. It is, indeed, characteristic of the ambitiousness of *Light in August* that it should contain within itself so many different fictional kinds, from the pastoral on the one hand to the detective story on the other.

The end of the first chapter – Lena's "My, my. A body does get around" (26) – creates its own strong closure, serving to mark off the opening sequence as a kind of prologue, ultimately to be balanced by the epilogue constituted by the novel's final and essentially comic return to Lena's gradual and unhurried progress through Mississippi and through life itself. Lena's biological compulsions, her irrepressible life force, are as universally valid as those evoked in Hardy's poem "In Time of 'the Breaking of Nations'":

> Yonder a maid and her wight
> Come whispering by:
> War's annals will cloud into night
> Ere their story die.[7]

That there is a contrastive relationship between Lena's story and Joe Christmas's story is obvious enough. But what is remarkable is the way in which Faulkner maintains the distinctiveness of each even when they appear to intersect. However extensively she may touch and affect the lives of others, the inherent simplicity and timelessness of Lena's own story – Lena's fable – enable it to remain essentially separate, a narrative within a narrative, even a narrative containing and framing a narrative. In *Light in August*, . indeed, it seems possible to speak of the presence side by side of a cast of comic characters – headed by Lena, Brown, and Byron Bunch – and a quite separate cast of tragic characters – chief among them Joe Christmas and Joanna Burden. What gives the novel its peculiar complexity is not just the suddenness of the shifts from the comic mode to the tragic and then back again but also the way in which members of the one group are sometimes transferred intact and unchanged into the territory of the other – as when Brown becomes clownishly involved in the desperate career of Christmas or the placidity of Lena and her baby is disturbed by the dangerous craziness of the Hineses. There is even an occasional superimposition of the two strands, as when Byron engages in his quixotic battle with the physically more powerful Brown at precisely the moment when Christmas is being shot and castrated by Percy Grimm.

It seems appropriate to speak of the two "strands" rather than of the two plots, chiefly because it is of the nature of Lena's story that it be essentially plotless and because *Light in August* (as Martin Kreiswirth demonstrates in his essay in this volume) so persistently refuses the interconnections and consolations and satisfactions that plots characteristically afford. But the term also has the advantage of giving a more precise sense of how the Lena Grove material and the Joe Christmas material actually relate to each other, as two strands intertwined throughout the text, bound together by a common setting and social context and by the overlapping of involved characters, but remaining nonetheless separate and distinct to the very end of the novel – at which point, as has often been observed, each strand is allowed its own entirely independent conclusion.

By beginning with Lena, Faulkner moves in with extraordinary and indeed deceptive gradualness upon the violent intensity of the central Joe Christmas narrative; by ending with her, he withdraws from that central narrative not with quite the same gradualness but with the similar effect of requiring the action as a whole to be viewed from a distanced perspective, seen within the context of the long history of humanity itself − a history as steady and as repetitious in terms of individual lives as the yearly progress of the seasons. Even within the novel, it becomes apparent that Joe Christmas is attempting to move toward the position represented by Lena − to get out of the detective novel and into the pastoral, to escape from the world of destructive violence into the peace and tranquility of mind that are represented by Lena and made vivid for Joe himself by his growing perception that the world and time itself may be different from what he had always assumed. His recognition that time is a "flat pattern," that "all that had ever been was the same as all that was to be" (266), actually precedes his murder of Miss Burden; it is during his flight from his pursuers that he experiences a still profounder moment of epiphany:

> It is just dawn, daylight: that gray and lonely suspension filled with the peaceful and tentative waking of birds. The air, inbreathed, is like spring water. He breathes deep and slow, feeling with each breath himself diffuse in the neutral grayness, becoming one with loneliness and quiet that has never known fury or despair. "That was all I wanted," he thinks, in a quiet and slow amazement. "That was all, for thirty years. That didn't seem to be a whole lot to ask in thirty years." (p. 313)

As a consequence of such moments of insight, Christmas's flight becomes in effect a journey toward self-knowledge, one that leads him eventually to give himself up and set in train the completion of that ritual of crime and punishment he had learned at the harsh hands of McEachern, his foster-father, many years before.

Hightower too, of course, is led directly by Lena to a new and at least temporary awareness of human continuity − *"The good stock peopling in tranquil obedience to it the good earth"* (384) − and it is tempting to think of the Hightower material as constituting a third strand plaited together throughout the text with the Lena Grove and Joe Christmas strands. To some extent, of course, such a characterization cannot be challenged. Especially in the latter stages of the novel, Hightower does emerge as a major figure, the subject of an internalized revaluation of his own past that is only less extensive and intensive than the more externalized recovery of Joe Christmas's past that occupies so many of the central chapters. And the Hightower fable – the representative narrative of a man who attempts to escape from a past-obsessed death-in-life – certainly takes a major place among the range of such fables offered by the book as a whole. But the quixotic fable of Byron Bunch also emerges strongly, and Hightower's role in the novel still seems to be governed by Faulkner's apparent conception of him as a narrative tool, a device for organizing a text that he intended from the first to be of unusual complexity and ambitiousness.

The evidence of the manuscript, combined with that of a manuscript fragment at the University of Texas, tends to suggest that Faulkner's original structural plan was to use Hightower, sitting for the most part immobile in his study, as the brooding and reflective recipient of narrative material that would necessarily be told or otherwise transmitted in flashbacks of various kinds – rather as the original version of *Sanctuary* had begun in mid-narrative, with Horace Benbow attempting to piece together the pattern of past events. It was a device that Faulkner had perhaps adapted from Conrad, and that he was to use with great effect in *Absalom, Absalom!*. The problem with such a method – brilliantly solved in *Absalom* by the introduction of Shreve McCannon – is that of maintaining narrative momentum during the periods when the past is being reassembled and of creating sufficient dramatic tension within the receiving and recording mind itself. What happens in *Light in August* as published is that a narrative line is set firmly in train before Hightower is introduced and that his principal reflections upon his own past are delayed until very late in the novel, when they can be seen in relation to the book's two major counterpointed actions – the death of Joe Christmas and the birth of Lena's baby – and when they can be used structurally as an element in the cadenced falling away and moving outward that follow upon the climactic intensity of Christmas's murder.

Hightower's reflectiveness, however, remains an essential element in Faulkner's self-conscious attempt to universalize the themes of the novel. Upon first hearing that Joe Christmas is being hunted for the murder of Miss Burden, Hightower exclaims, "Poor man. Poor mankind" (93). As the novel proceeds, he moves – like Christmas and Byron Bunch – in the direction of Lena and the forces and values she appears to represent, away from death and toward life, out from darkness into the light. And in the brooding chapter that intervenes, and in some sense holds the balance, between Christmas's tragic apotheosis and the final comic glimpse of Lena Grove in company with Byron Bunch, Hightower finally arrives at a compassionate vision of human interdependence that seems to draw together the more positive implications of the novel into something resembling a generalized statement.

The universality of the novel's themes is also established by the presence of a number of shadowy frames of religious or mythological reference – the implication, for example, of some sort of association between Lena Grove and the Virgin Mary, the suggestion that Joe Christmas *can* be viewed as Christlike in his victimization. At the same time, the crisis of identity experienced by Joe Christmas is treated with such amplitude and specificity that it emerges as at once an evocation and a fable of what has often been regarded as the universal modern condition. Faulkner seems always to have accepted the proposition, implicit in his entire creation and elaboration of Yoknapatawpha County, that universal themes may be most effectively presented through the intensive treatment of local and regional subject matter: Phil Stone's preface to Faulkner's very first book, *The Marble Faun,* had cited the dictum that "all universal art became great by first being provincial."[8] But *Light in August* disrupts the standard regionalist pattern, the conventions of modern pastoralism, by allowing the universal elements to emerge with directness and even with violence instead of by implication alone. At such a moment as Christmas's death, there is the sense, for almost the first time in Faulkner's work, of a passionate urgency thrusting in the direction of overt statement.

An explicit indication of the kind of creative ambition underlying the conception and composition of *Light in August* can be gained from the retrospective passage in which Faulkner attempted to evoke the experience of writing the novel in the wake of – and in the hope of repeating – the extraordinary creative ecstasy that had accompanied the writing of *The Sound and the*

40

Fury. That ecstasy did not return, he recalled, but its place was taken by a less spontaneous and less joyous yet no less imperious artistic self-consciousness and self-discipline: "I was now aware before each word was written down just what the people would do, since now I was deliberately choosing among possibilities and probabilities of behavior and weighing and measuring each choice by the scale of the Jameses and Conrads and Balzacs."[9] It becomes evident in the light of these remarks that in writing *Light in August* Faulkner set out to lay claim, once and for all, to the status of a major novelist – to measure himself quite specifically against such towering figures as Henry James, Joseph Conrad, and Honoré de Balzac – and to do so by making *Light in August* a work of stylistic eloquence, psychological depth, and magisterial scope, a "big" novel capable of standing alongside the greatest novels of the past.

It does not appear that Faulkner in *Light in August* felt himself to be specifically *indebted* to the novelists he mentioned, although it seems possible that Joanna Burden derives in part from James's Olive Chancellor and Joe Christmas from Razumov, the ambiguously presented, psychologically crippled, and quintessentially "lost" figure at the center of Conrad's *Under Western Eyes*: both Christmas and Razumov, of course, finally arrive at a kind of release or salvation by becoming the victims of sickening acts of physical brutality. The right Conrad novel, however, to invoke in this context – not necessarily as an influence but rather as a precedent, an incitement to emulation – is surely *Nostromo*, so rich in its sustained presentation of a whole series of parallel lives, so ambitious in its creation of an entire society, a visualizable fictional world, and so powerful in its evocation of a sense of historical depth underlying the social configurations and particular human crises of the present.

Nostromo is itself, of course, a novel that has sometimes been criticized as overlong, but there can be no doubt that its exceptional effectiveness as a sociohistorical fiction depends largely upon the way in which the "impressionistic" method – that sweeping backward and forward across broad stretches of time described by Ford Madox Ford as central to the approach to the novel he and Conrad had jointly developed[10] – allows for the apparently random revelation of additional facets of the past and present lives of individual characters (Pedrito Montero, Dr. Monygham, Charles Gould), as well as supplementary information about the history of Costaguana itself. It is also true that the narration and renarration of the same or similar events from a variety of different perspectives creates in the reader a quite exceptional density of conceptual apprehension, a sense of knowledge-in-depth that it is tempting to call stereoscopic.

It is possible to think of *Light in August* in similar terms, as a sociohistorical fiction constructed by means of discontinuous accretion rather than by a steady and sequential progression through chronological time. This is not simply a matter of the extended flashbacks and flashbacks-within-flashbacks, the most obvious instances of Faulkner's adaptation of Conradian impressionism. The disparate elements associated with particular characters or plot lines are continually flinging off exploratory probes into areas of time and space not previously mapped or documented in any way, and the information thus accumulated is not necessarily absorbed back into the novel's tripartite mainstream: the reader learns, for example, a good deal more about the ancestors of Hightower and Joanna Burden than seems essential to the recognition of a profound and unhappy kinship between the ostensibly opposed fanaticisms of South and North. For all of its detective-story aspects, the novel is not a disassembled jigsaw puzzle that the reader is required to fit together. Some mysteries are never decanted from their plots; several loose ends remain untied. If the truth of Christmas's birth is never known, neither can it be incontrovertibly determined that it was he who murdered Miss Burden and set fire to her house.[11]

To accept, however, that many things in *Light in August* remain unexplained, perhaps inexplicable, is not necessarily to assent to the thrust or even the integrity of the novel overall. The proliferating uncertainties of *Absalom, Absalom!* are specifically recognized for what they are, confronted as such by the different participants in the narrative process; "truth" is from the very beginning put in question, acknowledged to be multivalent, unstable, ultimately unattainable. But in *Light in August* it is only gradually that the reader learns to recognize that the explanations explicitly or implicitly offered for the pattern of events and the behavior of individuals are often exaggerated, biased, or simply incomplete, and that they are in any case likely to be enlarged upon, modified, or wholly contradicted by other explanations offered, either explicitly or implicitly, at other points in the text. Christmas, for example, is very differently perceived and understood by the reader at successive stages of the novel. Nor do those stages necessarily lead toward a final clarification. Although the reader's grasp of Christmas's situation and character is far richer and stronger at the end of the book than it was at the beginning of the second chapter, that enhanced understanding remains difficult to articulate, impossible to summarize in a simple formula or a single category, or, indeed, in any terms that are less than comprehensively reflective of the experience of reading the text in its entirety. The "truth" about Christmas is constituted precisely by the complexity of his presentation in the novel; it embraces, holds in suspension, all of those interpretations of his actions and insights into his psychology that have been offered along the way. None of them adequate in themselves, they nonetheless have each their own contribution to make to a continuing act of characterization that remains always in process, always (like Christmas himself) in motion, never attaining — except, perhaps, in the memories of Percy Grimm and his accomplices (440) — either the permanence or the coherence that might justify the use of such a term as "portrait."

In this, as in so much else, Christmas is obviously at the opposite extreme from Lena, whose past and present can be established in a page or two, whose individuality seems scarcely separable from her timeless representativeness, and whom it is therefore possible to think of as being captured forever as a figure in a landscape, an image on a vase. Closer to Christmas in terms of both the method and the complexity of her presentation is the character of Miss Burden. If Christmas's final actions confront the reader with a puzzle recalcitrant even to speculative solutions, so too do the final actions of Joanna Burden: Are they to be accounted for on physiological grounds ("It was not her fault that she got too old to be any good any more," says Joe, with a characteristic mix of compassion and brutality [99]), in terms of sheer emotional exhaustion, or as a resurgence of social and religious obsessions deriving from her upbringing and perhaps even from her heredity? As with Joe, no one of the explanations offered within the text seems sufficient by itself, and the reader is again thrown back upon a recognition of irreducible complexity – a recognition that calls sharply, even luridly, into question that automatic demand of the Jeffersonian community for a rigid categorization of those perceived as socially deviant.

More seems to be involved here, however, than a simple contrast between the public image and the private reality. Nor does the book seem necessarily to be saying that to know all is to forgive all. Whatever case might, or must, be made out for Joe Christmas, his habitual resort to violence constitutes a social threat that Byron Bunch's fellow workers at the planing mill were not wrong to identify. What *Light in August* does explore, with characteristic amplitude and force, is the central Faulknerian theme of the past's relation to the present, a relation seen as simultaneously ineluctable and intolerable – one from which society can never hope to free itself but from which the individual must never cease struggling to escape. The past-haunted, past-cursed, and past-determined characters of *Light in August* are set in motion within a world specifically contemporary with the moment of the novel's composition: Christmas dies and Lena's baby is born in August 1932. And Faulkner chose with equal deliberation, and with exceptional objectivity and courage, to explore the roots and confront the effects of contemporary Southern violence, racism, and vigilante lawlessness in terms certainly disturbing to his primarily northern and urban readership and presumably no less offensive (though for different reasons) to those few people from his own region who might happen to come across the book. On the one hand, as Cleanth Brooks has insisted, Jefferson's troubles originate with outsiders; on the other hand, it is precisely in terms of its capacity to cope with disruptive elements, both from without and from within, that any community must ultimately be judged. What *Light in August*, like most of Faulkner's novels, tends to suggest is that Jefferson, like most communities, offers its members a reassuring sense of group protection and cohesion, that it copes sometimes well and sometimes badly with strangers, that it contains both good and evil (often within a single character), and that its present is in any case impossible to understand without some knowledge of its past.

It is true that little attention is paid to the individual past lives or family backgrounds of the permanent inhabitants of Jefferson. The members of the community – variously invoked as "the people" or "they" or "the town" (59, 60), as "the women" (273) or, a little more specifically, as "the clerks, the idle, the countrymen in overalls" (330) – are characterized almost always as a group, essentially indistinguishable in terms of their backgrounds, their social and racial attitudes, and their religious beliefs. They con-stitute, after all, the sustaining context, the essential "given," of the entire structuring drama of social acceptance and rejection, and their responses to strangers – their tolerance of the un-threatening and familiar, their intolerance of the threatening and unfamiliar – are automatic and unexamined, wholly devoid of any awareness of historical context. What fascinated and concerned Faulkner were the causes and consequences of the differentness of the different, the alienation of the alienated. And it was his search for these that generated not just the long and intricate Joe Christ-mas flashback but also those briefer treatments of the backgrounds of Miss Burden and Hightower in which Faulkner – with superb ambition, intellectual sophistication, and structural skill – used the histories of Jefferson's intruders to invoke the history of Jefferson itself and the evolution of those contending religious and intellec-tual forces – Calvinism, abolitionism, separatism, racial prejudice – that helped to shape its contemporary rigidity.

It is through the ancestors of Miss Burden and Hightower that the novel touches upon, intersects with, the public history of the South, primarily during the periods of the Civil War and Recon-struction. These episodes are too short, and too fragmentary, to give *Light in August* the character of an historical novel, but they are sufficiently extended and powerful to constitute history, or at least the transmission of historical memory, as a determining fac-tor in the individual lives of Miss Burden and Hightower and as a powerful, if largely unconscious, influence upon the present-time actions and attitudes of the community at large. Significantly, the elements from the past that remain most influential are precisely those that themselves seem incomprehensible or demanding of explanation, as if Faulkner sought to demonstrate that behind the puzzling actions of the present may lie the no less inexplicable actions of the past, rendered the more haunting and persistent in memory (as Quentin Compson was to discover in *Absalom, Absalom!*) by the very fact of their absurdity or outrageousness. So Hightower is obsessed by the contrast between the splendor of his grandfather's gallantry and the pointless squalor of his death; so Joe Christmas finds himself appalled by the hatred and fear that induced Miss Burden's father to hide the graves of his father and son, shot in Jefferson by Colonel Sartoris just after the Civil War; so Miss Burden herself struggles to come to terms with the ambiguous fanaticism that is her family inheritance.

Within such a context, the recurrent Faulknerian insistence upon the need to break free from the dead hand of the past takes on an additional urgency. To see the past as itself devoid of value and meaning is to remove the last justification for its perpetuation in the present, and it seems significant that some of the most disastrous actions in *Light in August* are performed by those seeking to compensate for lives not lived: Miss Burden attempting to pursue vicariously through Joe the life of social action so largely denied her as a woman; Hightower blinding himself to the urgent needs of his wife and his flock in his almost sacrilegious commitment to the perpetual reenactment of his grandfather's death; Percy Grimm's provoking and performing acts of obscene violence in his desire to recapture a military past he has never in fact known.

It would be too much to say that *Light in August* projects a meaningless world: it is precisely the sense of human possibility and value that gives point and poignancy to the changes that occur within such characters as Christmas, Hightower, and Byron Bunch. At the same time, it is central to the essentially modernist challenge of the novel that its world should become a progressively more troubled and ambiguous place than it had appeared to be in its opening chapter, and correspondingly more taxing of the reader's capacity for moral discrimination and judgmental suspension. And at the very end of the book the reader is left not only with those narrative uncertainties identified by Martin Kreiswirth but with profound moral uncertainties as well. How far is the last chapter's apparently optimistic "flight into Egypt" image of mother, child, and potential but precuckolded husband qualified by our knowledge of the career of a child born at, and named for, Christmas? What exactly is it that Hightower has learned and (setting aside the minor uncertainty as to whether he lives or dies) how profoundly has it affected his perception of the world? To what extent, indeed, should it affect the reader's perception of Christmas's death and of the meaning of the novel as a whole? Why, for that matter, did Christmas give himself up and why, having done so, did he then run away once more? Several other questions cluster around the fate of Christmas: What did Mrs. Hines say to him when she visited him in prison? Did he knowingly run to Hightower's house?

The central issue of the potentially suicidal nature of Christmas's actions, projected outward as it is by the sheer power of Faulkner's description of the actual event, retains an urgency and permanence in the reader's imagination that is at least partly ascribable to the inexplicitness and incompleteness of the text itself. The obvious inadequacy of Gavin Stevens's interpretation of the events leading to Christmas's death serves only to draw attention to the fact that Faulkner's presentation of Christmas, rich as it is in so many respects, does not provide direct access to his thoughts at this crucial moment, nor at a number of other moments of scarcely less importance. Clearly, this constitutes not so much a failure of explanation on Faulkner's part as a deliberate withholding of explanation precisely in order to provoke imaginative participation by the reader — somewhat along the lines of Hemingway's more exclusively narrative conception of strengthening a story by omitting elements that the author had in fact comprehensively imagined. So Faulkner himself was later to declare that beauty was most effectively evoked by understatement, that "every man has a different idea of what's beautiful," and that it was therefore best for the writer "to take the gesture, the shadow of the branch, and let the mind create the tree."[12]

The novel's evocation of the world of Jefferson and, more broadly, of Yoknapatawpha County depends to some extent upon the same technique of fragmentary suggestion. By the time he came to write *Light in August*, Faulkner had already used Jefferson as a major setting in *Sartoris, The Sound and the Fury, As I Lay Dying, Sanctuary,* and a number of short stories. And since he was already embarked upon the creation of an integrated fictional world extending over a series of texts, he had necessarily to assume – or to allow for the possibility – that the readers of each new novel were already familiar with its predecessors. There are, indeed, repeated evocations of the rural landscape in the opening chapter of *Light in August,* but once the action moves to Jefferson itself, the settings of individual scenes tend to emerge not in advance of but in tandem with the dramatic presentations of those scenes, in terms not of set-piece descriptions but of unelaborated narrative details and unglossed allusions to other texts – most, although by no means all, of them previously published.

The Yoknapatawphan names Armstid, Grimm, Varner, and Winterbottom all occur in *Light in August;* Mr. Maxey reappears from the story "Hair," Captain McLendon from "Dry September," Mrs. Beard from *Sartoris;* Buck Conners, already introduced in "Centaur in Brass," will return, renamed Connors, in *The Town;* Gavin Stevens, previously established in "Hair" and "Smoke," will eventually become perhaps the most important of all of Faulkner's recurrent characters; the episode of Colonel Sartoris's shooting of Joanna Burden's grandfather and brother will be treated at greater length, and from a quite different point of view, in the story "Skirmish at Sartoris" and, later, in *The Unvanquished.* As in *Sartoris,* but with much greater subtlety and force, the Jefferson of the novel's present is linked with events from its own past and thus acquires something of the historical depth and multidimensional solidity that Faulkner sought to achieve for his fictional world as a whole.

Precedents for *Light in August*'s powerful combination of density of treatment with largeness of scale can, of course, be found in all three of the earlier novelists invoked by Faulkner – in Balzac and, to a lesser extent, in James, as well as in Conrad. Critics have often been reminded, too, of the work of Charles Dickens when contemplating the large scale of *Light in August,* its social sweep, its range of significantly named characters, its alternating narratives, its broad symbolic effects and strongly contrasted patterns of imagery, and the book's first chapter, in which Lena Grove makes her

48

placid way across the landscape of northern Mississippi, has been found reminiscent of the topographical openings of Thomas Hardy's fiction, of novels such as *The Return of the Native* and *The Mayor of Casterbridge*. But if *Light in August* gives an initial impression of relative conventionality, the features distinguishing it from Faulkner's technically more spectacular texts have little real connection with the actual methods of his admired predecessors. There is, above all, a profound difference between the tight and comprehensive plotting characteristic of nineteenth-century fiction and the much looser organization of *Light in August* in terms of that judicious disposition of large narrative blocks that Faulkner had by this time already recognized as the governing principle of his structural method.

Immediately before writing *Light in August*, Faulkner had devised for the group of entirely discrete narratives included in the short story collection *These 13* the kind of organization that he was later to describe as "contrapuntal in integration,"[13] and it seems particularly significant that in his letter thanking Harrison Smith for sending a copy of the first edition of *Light in August*, Faulkner mentioned that in putting together the collection of his verse that was shortly to be published under the title *A Green Bough*, he had simply chosen what he thought were the best poems "and built a volume just like a novel."[14] Faulkner was fond of describing the achievements of the literary artist in terms of the constructive skills of the carpenter; the metaphor of building was profoundly important to him – building, that is to say, as practiced in places where houses are typically assembled plank by plank or brick by brick; and there is every reason to think of *Light in August* as having been put together, block by block, as if from the ground up, with much shifting around of individual blocks until the point could be found at which they would best fit together with the blocks already in place.

It was, indeed, its elaboration and confirmation of this constructive method that probably constituted the chief importance of *Light in August* in relation to Faulkner's subsequent career. He had attempted something similar before, most notably in *Sartoris* and *Sanctuary* and in short stories such as "Dry September." In *Sartoris*, however, even in its full *Flags in the Dust* version, there is a lack of overall conceptual coherence: because Faulkner seems not to have determined his structural priorities, he fails to reconcile his concern for social representation – the creation of a persuasive image of a particular society at a particular moment in time – with the establishment and development of either his major or his minor characters. And in *Sanctuary* the introjected chapters – the early Memphis experiences of those corrupted innocents Virgil and Fonzo, the grotesque celebration of Red's funeral – seem too independent of each other to establish a pattern or rhythm for the novel as a whole.

It was in *Light in August* that Faulkner first successfully found his way to a structure within which narratives kept essentially distinct and separate in plot terms could nonetheless be so deployed as to ensure their constant interreaction – each persistently modifying the other(s) in some way, generally with ironic or even parodic consequences. Byron Bunch's fight with Brown, for example, was spoken of earlier as superimposed upon the moment of Christmas's death, but it might be alternatively suggested that Byron's deliberate choice of victimization in his conflict with Brown – he knows from the start that he is going to be bested and badly beaten in the struggle – is in some sense a parodic commentary on Christmas's choice of victimization at the hands of Percy Grimm. The organization of the novel around a series of salient incidents or recurrent patterns – such as the burning of Miss Burden's house, the arrest of Joe Christmas, and the exposition of the ancestry of the central characters – gives ample opportunity for such interreflections between narratives to occur, and Faulkner often uses them to amplify both his psychological and his social themes. Think, for instance, of the contrasted responses of the people of Jefferson to that series of intruders with whom the novel is centrally concerned, or of the determining roles played by grandfathers in the lives of Christmas, Hightower, and Miss Burden.

Faulkner, in fact, seems to have been attempting in *Light in August* essentially the same kind of contrapuntal relationship that he later precipitated out, so to speak, in the double novel entitled *The Wild Palms,* in which the separation of the narratives is still more radically enforced. It is also possible to argue that a similar structural principle is operative in *Requiem for a Nun,* and that it was his realization of the specifically social implications of such a method – the way in which it could be made to subserve the evocation of a functioning community – that enabled Faulkner to find a way of bringing together some of his disparate Snopes narratives into, first, *The Hamlet* and, later, *The Town* and *The Mansion*. In *The Hamlet* the separate blocks of material are, indeed, provided with loose narrative links, but they are at the same time distinguished from one another with particular sharpness by their very considerable stylistic differences. Above all, *Light in August* can be seen as the direct ancestor of *Go Down, Moses*, the novel of Faulkner's that is perhaps most clearly and most successfully constructed by means of the assembly and effective deployment of large and virtually independent narrative blocks.

By the same token, *Light in August* can be said to look forward still further to *A Fable*, perhaps the one novel for which Faulkner's conscious aspirations were even greater than they had been for *Light in August* itself. *A Fable*, of course, was a work so elaborately constructed out of separate blocks that Faulkner had to draw a chart on his study wall to help him keep track of them; it was also, like *Light in August*, a novel in which the numerous parallel narratives were developed largely on account of their potentiality as independent fables of the human condition. Moreover, the story of the stolen racehorse is incorporated into *A Fable* in a manner directly comparable to the handling of the long Joe Christmas flashback in *Light in August*, and the Melvillean trinity of conscience that Faulkner spoke of as central to *A Fable* – "knowing nothing, knowing but not caring, knowing and caring"[15] – can be seen as having been anticipated in the earlier novel by the respective positions of Lena Grove, Gail Hightower, and Byron Bunch.

These are broad and general speculations, very much open to question and challenge. If, however, one returns finally to the text of *Light in August* itself, there seems no question but that the process of assembling and disposing the novel's many narrative blocks was carried out – as the manuscript reveals – with immense care and deliberation and without the slightest hint of carelessness or casualness on Faulkner's part. His handling of the book's intricate chronology displays what Stephen Meats has called an "astonishing precision,"[16] and the acknowledged technical brilliance of novels such as *As I Lay Dying* and *Absalom, Absalom!* leaves no room for thinking that Faulkner had simply failed to find appropriate ways of restricting the independent growth of the various *Light in August* narratives and binding them more closely together. Clearly, he deliberately chose that the structure of the novel not be more tightly controlled. Clearly, he wanted the different narrative strands to develop at their appropriate pace and length in order that they might make their own full and independent statements as fables of the human condition. But that did not prevent their responding to one another within the text itself, nor did it in any way impair that text's status as a novel.

Faulkner wrote *Light in August* in the imagined presence of those great novelists whom he admired and sought to emulate for the sheer quality and quantity of their life's work, their demonstration of what the novel and the novelist could at their highest levels attain. Although *Light in August* may have begun with nothing more substantial than the image of Lena Grove walking along a country road, it became under Faulkner's shaping hands an expansive, expressively structured, and highly self-conscious literary artifact, powerfully written, rich in every sort of narrative detail, solidly regional in its setting but eloquent of some of the fundamental psychological and psychic crises of its time. Not just an anecdote, as Faulkner said, but a novel, and not just a novel either but a major twentieth-century text with an importance in Faulkner's perception of his own career that was perhaps equaled only by one earlier novel, *The Sound and the Fury,* and one later, that even more ambitiously conceived and executed work he called, quite explicitly, *A Fable.*

NOTES

1. *Selected Letters of William Faulkner,* ed. Joseph Blotner (New York: Random House, 1977), p. 66.
2. *Lion in the Garden: Interviews with William Faulkner 1926–1962,* ed. James B. Meriwether and Michael Millgate (New York: Random House, 1968), p. 31.
3. John B. Cullen and Floyd C. Watkins, *Old Times in the Faulkner Coun-*

try (Chapel Hill: University of North Carolina Press, 1961), pp. 89–98.

4. The character was called Plunkett in the magazine version of "Dry September," but the change of name had occurred in *These 13*, published in September 1931.
5. See Michael Millgate, *The Achievement of William Faulkner* (London: Constable, 1966), p. 111.
6. "A Note on *Sanctuary*," *Harvard Advocate*, November 1951, p. 16.
7. *The Complete Poetical Works of Thomas Hardy*, ed. Samuel Hynes, (Oxford: Clarendon Press, 1984), Vol. II, p. 296.
8. *The Marble Faun* (1924; reprint, with *A Green Bough*, New York: Random House, 1965), p. 7.
9. "An Introduction for *The Sound and the Fury*," ed. James B. Meriwether, *Southern Review* n.s. 8 (Autumn 1972):709.
10. Ford, *Joseph Conrad: A Personal Remembrance* (London: Duckworth, 1924), especially p. 130.
11. See Stephen E. Meats, "Who Killed Miss Burden?" *Mississippi Quarterly* 24 (Summer 1971):271–7.
12. Meriwether and Millgate, eds., *Lion in the Garden*, p. 128.
13. Blotner, ed., *Selected Letters*, p. 278.
14. Ibid., p. 67.
15. Meriwether and Millgate, eds., *Lion in the Garden*, p. 247.
16. "The Chronology of *Light in August*," in *William Faulkner's "Light in August": A Critical Casebook*, ed. François Pitavy (New York: Garland, 1982), p. 227.

3

Plots and Counterplots: The Structure of *Light in August*

MARTIN KREISWIRTH

F ROM the first reviews to some of the most recent articles, critics of *Light in August* have been anxious about the novel's structure. Praise of its characterization, themes, language, mythic strength, and so on, has been characteristically given despite an acknowledged formal instability. Disturbing the numerous accolades the novel has received is an audible undercurrent of critical doubt: Where is its structural coherence? What of its unity? Is there wholeness? Comprehensive design? The question of the novel's narrative structure has invaded, tacitly or openly, almost every discussion of the text, avowedly formalist or not.

Light in August is a text whose narrative structure calls attention to itself, although not in such terms as symmetrical balance (as in *The Ambassadors*), architechtonics (as in *Tom Jones*), or *progression d'effet* (as in *Madame Bovary*). The novel does not, in fact, project wholeness, but precisely its opposite, positively flaunting its disunity, structural lapses, digressions, asymmetries, and imbalances. Its very narrative form, its overall structure, questions some of the genre's most cherished conventions: the expectations that the text will contain a single, unified (Aristotelian) plot, identifiable protagonists, and, perhaps most insistently, formal wholeness. But, at the same time, *Light in August* also rhetorically assures us that its broken and lopsided organization – Faulkner, at one point, called it "topheavy"[1] – is indeed some kind of an organization and not an accident or miscalculation: there is an inconsistent but insistent pull toward interaction, dialogue, and mutual attention. This fundamental doubleness calls into question the overall structure of the text – "problematizes" it, to use the current term – and is responsible for both critical anxiety and critical attention.

55

Formal heterogeneity is, of course, a characteristic feature of the Faulknerian text. Practically all of his works are structurally discontinuous, technically fragmented, and composed of diverse, almost self-contained parts. Individual novels are made up of sections that contain different narrative perspectives (*The Sound and the Fury, As I Lay Dying*), different styles (*Absalom, Absalom!, The Hamlet*), different genres (*Requiem for a Nun*), different lines of action (*The Wild Palms, Go Down, Moses,* and, of course, *Light in August* itself), and different combinations of these elements. They are, in the widest sense, what Mikhail Bakhtin calls "many-voiced" or "polyphonic."[2] It seems at bottom, in fact, that Faulkner viewed fictional construction in terms of the fitting together of different (and sometimes disparate) units of narrative discourse. Form in these texts, then, is multiple and dynamic rather than singular and fixed. And structure resides in patterns of juxtaposition, parallelism, montage, and counterpoint.

That Faulkner frequently wrote with these principles in mind is clear from his public statements. He spoke many times, for example, of "counterpointing" and "dovetailing" the two "antithetical" stories of *The Wild Palms*, of the "contrapuntal effect" of the narratively and stylistically autonomous interludes of *Requiem for a Nun*, and of "fitting the bricks" of *As I Lay Dying* "neatly together."[3] Faulkner's comments on the structure of *Light in August* are similar. When, during the 1957 class conferences at the University of Virginia, he was asked why he had placed the chapter about Hightower's early life at the end of the book, he responded in terms that point toward these basic concepts of form:

> Unless a book follows a simple direct line such as a story of adventure, it becomes a series of pieces. It's a good deal like dressing a showcase window. It takes a certain amount of judgment and taste to arrange the different pieces in the most effective place in juxtaposition to one another. That was the reason. It seemed to me that was the most effective place to put that, to underline the tragedy of Christmas's story by the tragedy of his antithesis.[4]

Though Faulkner's metaphor for literary construction ("dressing a showcase window") may seem unduly restrictive and modest (like his similar use of the "carpentering" metaphor elsewhere), it does clearly emphasize that he saw this activity, particularly with regard to *Light in August,* as primarily concerned with the placement, juxtaposition, and arrangement of separate, formally distinct "pieces." This procedure, in fact, is also corroborated by the existing evidence about the actual composition of the novel.[5]

The contrapuntal method of *Light in August* forces the text's multiple elements to work dialectically; during the reading process the individual parts – stories, characters, themes – constantly combine, break apart, and then recombine in new configurations. The reader is put in an active, structuring role: he or she is confronted with difference not coherence, multiplicity not unity, dialogue not monologue (to use Bakhtin's terms), and must pull together materials, locate connections, and perceive similarities and dissimilarities. The different "pieces," moreover, do not achieve a progressive synthesis, but move rather toward a kind of uneasy suspension or temporary accord. Viewed in this way, the text thus opens up, and indeed rhetorically emphasizes, ambiguities, instabilities, and tensions.

At the same time, however (and this is, again, what problematizes the formal structure), the text's openness is inhibited and somewhat neutralized by its stress on interaction: the various narrative parts, as many critics have noted, work with each other as well as against each other. Along with the horizontal arrangement of the seemingly separable narrative blocks is a vertical insistence on recurrence, analogy, and simultaneity. Together with the obvious spatial and temporal links (Lena's lying-in in Christmas's cabin; Christmas's death in Hightower's house, etc.) and the complex biographical patterns of identity and difference that abstractly connect the major characters (e.g., Christmas and Lena are both orphans, having left their adoptive families through windows; Hightower and Joanna are both long-standing pariahs, etc.), one finds repetitions of images (e.g., shoes, corridors), phrases (both Hines and McEachern are fond of confronting women with "Jezebel!"), and actions (Christmas and his grandfather, Doc Hines, both break into black churches, etc.), as well as the presentation of simultaneous events (Grimm encounters Christmas at the same moment as Byron encounters Lena; Lena and Joanna both discover their pregnancies at the same time). The sequentially experienced, centrifugal movement toward fragmentation and instability is thus seemingly countered and held in check by a cumulative, centripetal pull toward interrelation; the discontinuities we confront progressively are modified to some extent by the continuities we perceive retrospectively. Structure in this sense becomes an exercise in balance, an adjustment of force and counterforce that plays what we are just now discovering against what we have already come to know, keeping the volatile materials of the novel just below the flashpoint.

To examine how the ordering of materials in *Light in August* affects the reader's progressive apprehension of its structure, it seems appropriate to start where this process starts – at the text's beginning. Openings of novels serve several important functions. They generally offer expository materials that introduce and orient the reader to the composition of the fictional world – the time period, setting, central characters. They also establish certain "contracts" with the reader, emphasizing information about generic conventions (does the fictional world conform to the physical laws of our world? etc.) and stylistic and rhetorical norms (metaphoric density, point of view, etc.).

Openings, moreover, leave important information out; they open gaps that the text promises to fill. These various promises work to keep the reader reading and, together with their partial resolutions and reformulations, constitute what Roland Barthes calls the text's "hermeneutic" code.[6] Each instability or indeterminacy of this type pushes the reader toward some tentative hypothesis or, in the language of "reception theory," some "horizon of expectation" that controls, for a time, the way in which subsequent data are arranged and interpreted.[7]

Yet, it is at the text's opening that these horizons are first defined and – because fictional discourse is necessarily processed over time, sequentially – it is here that they exert the most force. As Meir Sternberg has persuasively demonstrated, one's first impressions of a novel tend to dominate one's subsequent response: initial formulations, attitudes, and expectations potently influence the way in which later materials are apprehended and interrelated.[8] This "primacy effect," as many novelists themselves have realized, gives openings preponderant rhetorical prominence and – together with the unavoidable psychological difficulties that underlie beginnings – makes starting a text a vastly complex and problematic undertaking.

It is therefore not surprising to discover that Faulkner seems to have had some difficulty in finding a satisfactory opening for *Light in August*. Although he stated, in 1933, that the novel originated, as the published book does, with Lena Grove,[9] textual evidence reveals a different story. However accurately Faulkner's account might describe the novel's imaginative genesis, the actual writing seems to have taken a rather circuitous route (analogous to the larger frame structure of the entire book) before it returned to a presentation of Lena. The prepublication documents reveal not only that the initial pages are among the most heavily revised but that during composition Faulkner shifted various blocks of material into the beginning position; at different times, in fact, the novel seems to have begun with each of the other narrative strands – with Hightower's biography (now chapter 3) and with Christmas's capture (chapter 15 in the published book).[10]

The problem of the novel's opening thus reflects and, in a sense, duplicates the larger problem of its overall structure. Faulkner's choosing to begin (or rebegin, if indeed this is where the text truly originated in his imagination) with the chapter that introduces Lena and describes her journey toward Jefferson suggests that he wanted the reader to build the fictional construct upon this foundation. Although, as we shall see, the prominence of Lena's narrative position is significantly weakened after the early expository chapters, her story, and indeed her ethos, dominate the initial and therefore most privileged formulation of the novel's projected world. Here the hermeneutic code is centered upon Lena; the reader's expectations, questions, and concerns deal almost exclusively with her plight. Even after Christmas comes to the fore during the middle of the book, even after his tortured chronicle of "blood" and "violence" violates, as it were, her "pastoral,"[11] Lena's narrative succeeds in reasserting its primacy, ultimately to regain its formally commanding position at the novel's close. Indeed, the opening emphasis on Lena begins a process of foregrounding that ensures that even though her narrative may be temporarily suspended or hidden, it will always resurface.

Faulkner goes to great lengths to encode this hermeneutic

prominence right from the novel's opening pages. Many of Faulkner's works, as I have argued elsewhere, ignore exposition and begin, rather, with confused and fragmented previews of the book's thematic elements: in *The Sound and the Fury*, for example, the reader is greeted with Benjy's chaotic discourse, which provides little expository information but, by obsessively revolving around images of death and loss, distinctly prefigures the text's central concerns.[12] But in *Light in August*, Faulkner eschews his characteristically experimental and disorienting opening strategies and begins in more traditional fashion with an almost standard introduction of character and plot. Although certain important thematic elements are indeed obliquely introduced in the first chapter of *Light in August* – for example, the use of shoes as an index of social or public roles (for Lena here and for Christmas later) and of names as a determinant of identity ("I told you false. My name is not Burch yet. It's Lena Grove" [15]; "*My name aint McEachern. My name is Christmas*" [136]) – it is clear that in this text Faulkner wanted the primacy effect to establish plot and character rather than theme. Indeed, in this chapter, as in the following two, conventional exposition is stressed: after a paragraph that establishes the action – Lena's journey – already in progress and the time and place of the fictive present (through present-tense verbs), we are immediately offered three pages that provide the "specific antecedents indispensable" to an understanding of this action.[13] This summary narrative (in the past tense) covers about nine years and emphasizes only those details that explain Lena's present predicament and its potential resolution.

Thus, at the very opening of chapter 1, the reader is initially confronted with what Sternberg calls "preliminary exposition."[14] This concentrated block of explanatory material appears before the development of the narrative proper and posits its origins: Lena is on the road, we learn, *because* she is pregnant, has an unsympathetic (adoptive) family, and hopes to find and indeed marry the father of her child (1–4). We discover a little later (6, 9), moreover, that she has recently heard that her lover, Lucas Burch, is working in Jefferson, information that serves to link the expository material causally and temporally with the action of the fictive present – her journey to that town.

Practically everything in this rhetorically privileged first chapter points to the development of a single-stranded, traditional plot that raises expectations about the plight of a central character. The plot's initial formulation is straightforward: Lena's action in the present develops logically and unambiguously out of known details from her past. (There are, indeed, no hermeneutic gaps in her biography; throughout the remainder of the book the reader learns virtually nothing more about her background than what is presented here at the very beginning.) The plot is also what Austin Wright has called *dynamic:* it builds upon an instability whose resolution would involve a change in the fictional world – the discovery of Burch – not upon a disclosure of as yet unknown information.[15] And it is, seemingly, a comic plot: there is an ironic disparity between the community's view of the possible outcome of the situation and Lena's hopelessly naive expectations, as well as the fact that its potential resolution – her finding of Lucas and their marriage – would involve the conventionally comic re-establishment of the family unit.

As the chapter ends, the initial instability, again in typical fashion, is further complicated. New narrative expectations are created by the information that "that fellow in Jefferson at the planing mill is named Bunch and not Burch" (21–2). This development keeps the plot opened up to fresh possibilities and directs the reader to posit questions about the whereabouts of Lucas Burch, the identity of Bunch, and the outcome of Lena's travels. The opening chapter's emphatic push toward motion and future discovery, moreover, is underscored by Faulkner's curious shifting of verb tenses – undoubtedly the most experimental aspect of this otherwise rather conventional narrative induction. Here, retrospective explanations (the expository summary of Lena's past) and actions not dominated by Lena's presence (Armstid's dealings with Winterbottom) are narrated, for the most part, in past-tense forms, whereas ongoing actions centered on Lena and her movement toward Jefferson and her destiny are given the immediacy and narrative drive of the present tense.

Yet, as strongly as chapter 1 stresses Lena's plot and the expectations that derive from it, chapter 2 just as strongly sustains, even while it suspends, these expectations by offering a series of other preliminary expositions, focused on the arrivals in Jefferson of other and, as yet, unrelated characters. Even though the only immediate connections between chapter 1 and the opening of chapter 2 are Bunch's name and the continued use of the present tense (at least for the first sentence), the overriding convention of narrative coherence combines with the emphasis on Lena in the earlier chapter to force the reader to try to relate the materials of chapter 2 to her plot. Since these seem at odds with the developing action, the expository introductions of Christmas (27–32) and Brown (32–42) work largely to create suspense. They function, first of all, as narrative gaps or delays, postponing the progress of Lena's search by interrupting it with as yet unassimilated data. At the same time, they offer information that *may* be relevant to the established plot, information that is therefore perceived as potentially useful, latent, or, to use Roman Ingarden's term, "held in readiness."[16] As a result of Faulkner's prior stress on Lena's narrative, the reader attempts to place these various new beginnings within an encompassing "horizon of expectations": How, we are tacitly led to ask, will the Christmas and Brown materials be linked up with Lena's quest?

This retroactive and cumulative pull toward connection, however, is simultaneously countered, in chapter 2, by a push in a new narrative direction. Here Faulkner begins to complicate and call into question what up to now has been processed as a linear, Aristotelian plot, with a beginning, comprising the expository material on Lena, and the initiation of a "middle," where the materials of the beginning are destabilized. But the summary introductions of Christmas and Brown not only offer totally new and discontinuous information, they also arouse a new and seemingly discontinuous set of narrative expectations. Superimposed now on the dynamic plot, which moves forward in time toward some situational change – Lena's comic search – is what Wright calls a *disclosure* plot, which moves backward in time toward the discovery of some already existing but hidden aspect of the fictional world.[17] The expository descriptions first of Christmas's and then of Brown's arrivals in Jefferson are totally unlike the depiction of Lena's arrival in that practically everything remains hidden and mysterious; every rhetorical device points toward information that is ambiguous, obscure, and only very gradually disclosed.

Christmas, for example, is first presented through a discourse that projects him as a virtual walking oxymoron. He is perceived by the community in terms of a series of enigmatic contradictions that are tossed back and forth by means of coordinating "yet nots" and "buts":

> He looked like a tramp, *yet not* like a tramp either. His shoes were dusty and his trousers were soiled too. *But* they were of decent serge, sharply creased, and his shirt was soiled *but* it was a white shirt, and he wore a tie and a stiffbrim straw hat that was quite new, cocked at an angle arrogant and baleful above his still face. He did not look like a professional hobo in his professional rags, *but* there was something definitely rootless about him, as though no town nor city was his, no street, no walls, no square of earth his home. (p. 27; my emphases)

His name also functions as a kind of as yet undisclosed cipher: "[A]s soon as they heard it, it was as though there was something in the sound of it that was trying to tell them what to expect"; "And that was the first time Byron remembered that he had ever thought how a man's name, which is supposed to be just the sound for who he is, can be somehow an augur of what he will do, if other men can only read the meaning in time" (29).

Although Brown's origins, too, remain as yet unintelligible, his narrative induction stresses secrecy rather than obscurity. Thus, his name appears to be an alias (rather than a cryptogram): "There was no reason why his name should not have been Brown. It was that, looking at him, a man would know that at some time in his life he would reach some crisis in his own foolishness when he would change his name, and that he would think of Brown to change it to with a kind of gleeful exultation, as though the name had never been invented" (33). And he is evoked in terms of a series of metaphors — a driverless car with a blaring radio (32–3), a worthless horse (33) — rather than of oxymorons.

The use of Byron's admittedly limited narrative perspective to introduce these characters necessarily keeps many crucial facts hidden. Unlike the full disclosure of Lena's past presented through the perspective of the authoritative external narrator, the introductions of Christmas and Brown are full of acknowledged gaps: "No one knew where he lived" (31); "They still do not know for certain . . ." (41); "some of them know . . . [b]ut even these do not know" (42). Moreover, Faulkner sets up the temporal disposition of the narrative so that everything that the reader learns about Christmas and Brown – initially prefaced by "Byron Bunch knows this:" (27) – turns out to be only partial knowledge ("This is just what he knew then, what he heard and watched as it came to his knowledge" [31]) and is presented as pointing to some as yet undisclosed event in the fictive present ("what Byron knows now" [31]) that is not in fact revealed for several chapters.

Thus, with the introductions of Christmas and Brown, Faulkner progressively diverts and reroutes the novel's initial, dynamic line of action – Lena's search for her estranged lover – by grafting on to it a disclosure plot that alters, at least temporarily, the reader's developing horizon of expectations. Now, as well as desiring to know the outcome of Lena's quest, the reader wants to discover exactly what it is these mysterious men have done. As in the earlier plot, however, Faulkner complicates this developing secondary line of action and retains suspense by offering certain narrative satisfactions – only, at those points, to bring forward new gaps and expectations.

This can be seen, for example, in the manner in which Byron's narrative orders and interconnects the Christmas and Brown stories. The chapter's first five pages focus exclusively on Christmas's contradictory and enigmatic nature and lead the reader to ask basic biographical questions. Yet, as soon as some details begin to emerge – we learn authoritatively that "behind the veil, the screen, of his negro's job at the mill" he carried on as a bootlegger and lived "in a tumble down negro cabin on Miss Burden's place" (31–2) – disclosure stops. Instead of moving on to discover more about the basic narrative questions, the overriding hermeneutic ("what Byron knows now"), the reader is thrown back to the past and forced to attend to more exposition: the story of the arrival at the mill of "another stranger" (Brown). At this point, in fact, Faulkner stresses the narrative gap, emphatically calling attention to the newness and distinctiveness of Brown's introduction by subverting common linguistic conventions of "given" and "new" information. Even though the reader has just been introduced to "the other stranger, Brown" in the immediately preceding paragraph (31–2), Brown is now presented as if he had not been referred to before – "Then one day about six months ago another stranger appeared at the mill" (32). Since the "other stranger" has already been defined as Brown, this new "stranger" is naturally first perceived as a different character; furthermore, Byron keeps this gap open, leaving the figure nameless, referring to him only by pronouns for more than a full page, before his name (Brown), and thus his connection with previous information, is revealed (33).

As soon as this gap is closed, however, and the newly integrated Christmas–Brown narrative begins to approach the fictive present, forward progress again ceases, and the reader is given another expository detour into the past. We learn not about the mysterious present doings of Christmas and Brown but about the personal past of yet "another stranger," Joanna Burden, a character who seems only superficially connected to the bootleggers – no one knows if she knows that they live in a cabin on her place (42) – and totally unconnected to Lena, but around whom a new mystery and a fresh set of expectations are immediately projected: "[I]t still lingers about her and about the place: something dark and outlandish and threatful" (42). At this point, when instabilities move toward further instabilities rather than toward resolutions and hermeneutic proliferation seems to have totally displaced narrative development, the disclosure plot reaches a cul-de-sac and there is a physical (visual) break in the text (42).

In the new section, exposition ceases: we return to the fictive present, resume the progressive temporal motion that we left off at the end of chapter 1, return to the present tense, and learn about Lena's arrival at the planing mill (just as we had learned about Christmas's and Byron's arrivals earlier in this chapter). Now the dynamic search plot regains ascendancy and reclaims the reader's interest by the introduction of yet another complication: Byron's love for Lena (42–4). This narrative ascendancy becomes, at least temporarily, a hegemony when, in the process of discussing the fire at the Burden place (a seemingly irrelevant detail that has been alluded to previously), Byron inadvertently lets out enough details about Brown to enable Lena, and the reader, to ascertain that he is in fact Lucas Burch, the absconded father of her child. This information prompts a retrospective realignment of the Christmas–Brown material, revealing its place in Lena's again dominant plot. The initial mystery (the whereabouts of Lena's lover) is now resolved, and the way in which Faulkner presents this – disclosing not the solution but merely the clues leading to the solution ("the little white scar," etc., [51]) – allows the reader the particular narrative satisfaction of closing this central hermeneutic gap himself.

Thus, just as the information about Christmas and Brown forced the reader retrospectively to reassess the previous information about Lena's journey and to posit, at least temporarily, a revised horizon of expectations, so the reintroduction of Lena's plot here provokes a move in the opposite direction. What began to appear like a new and disruptive sequence of actions, with a distinctive narrative thrust directed toward disjunction and disclosure, turns out, it seems, to be essentially only a detour, another development of the initial plot's "middle" stage. Along with this provisional resolution, moreover, we get, in proper Aristotelian fashion, the concomitant creation of new complications – Burch's obvious indifference and the problems his occupation might cause, as well as Byron's "interfering" love. By the end of chapter 2, therefore, the various seemingly disparate narrative lines appear to be cohering and propelling the novel toward the further development of an integrated, dynamic plot.

Chapter 3, however, once again reverses expectations. And it does so with a vengeance. Instead of moving forward, instead of finding narrative continuity, progression, and synthesis, the reader is thrown back into the past and confronted with discontinuous and retrogressive exposition. The chapter's eighteen pages focus exclusively on public knowledge of a heretofore ancillary character, the Reverend Hightower (mentioned previously on p. 43), and they chronicle, through a kind of corporate town voice filtered through Byron's consciousness, the almost twenty-five years he has lived in Jefferson in disgrace. The chapter is entirely biographical exposition. There is virtually no action in the fictive present, no connection with previous materials (except through the use of

Byron as recipient of the story), and no projection of new narrative instabilities – with the exception of the chapter's very last sentence, which returns the reader to action in the present.

Chapter 3, however, does have an important role to play and works with chapters 1 and 2 to help condition the reader to the particular reading strategies that are necessary for the apprehension of the text as a whole. Although it absolutely suspends development of the seemingly cumulative plot, it reasserts – and contributes substantially to – the ongoing establishment of a larger pattern of connection/disconnection of which the creation of an amalgamated, apparently central plot is only a part. The opening three chapters establish a dialectic of expectations and frustrations that depends upon the conditioning of the reader to switch between exposition/action, dynamic/disclosure plot structures, related/unrelated characters, public/private information, and past/present temporal perspectives. These chapters all function primarily as exposition, yet they not only serve independently to introduce the basic materials of the narrative, they also work together, as a kind of expository block, to orient the reader to the text's methods of formally disposing of these materials and, perhaps most significantly, to the demanding reading procedures that these methods entail. They serve to acclimatize the reader to the seesawing back and forth between those actions capable of being apprehended and explained as narratives and those that refuse such closure, and also to the various ways of processing these different kinds of discourse. They establish not a singular, authoritative voice and narrative strategy – "monologic," in Bakhtin's terms – but a dialogue of voices, actions, and strategies. The next chapter recapitulates, intensifies, and, most importantly, begins to provide reasons for this "dialogical" formal methodology.

The opening of chapter 4, unlike those of the first three chapters, does not mark a new beginning but develops directly out of previous materials. It has the same spatial and temporal setting (Hightower's house, Sunday evening) as the end of chapter 3 and continues the same action (the meeting between Hightower and Byron). Moreover, Byron's narrative (which constitutes virtually the entire chapter) directly links up with and follows from the events described at the end of chapter 2 (his meeting with Lena at the mill). Initially, everything in this chapter points toward continuity and interrelation: as Byron gradually and elliptically tells Hightower what transpired on the previous day, connections are made and gaps are filled in, so that much of the information "held in readiness" from the earlier expository passages can now be activated, ordered, and integrated. And the stress here on relation and synthesis, of course, fits what we have begun by now to anticipate as a characteristic pattern: following the disconnected, retrogressive, expository chapter 3, we return, in chapter 4, to an emphatic reassertion of narrative linkage and progressive development.

In this chapter, moreover, Faulkner stresses the interpretative processes involved in this linkage by having Hightower act as what Gerald Prince has called a "narratee."[18] He is not only the recipient of Byron's narrative but also functions as a model for the reader by explicitly calling attention to the means of making the narrative meaningful. For example, when Byron tells Hightower of the difficulty he has had (because of the commotion in town brought on by the fire) in trying to keep Lena from hearing more than he wants her to about her estranged lover, Hightower replies: "The house that burned yesterday. But I dont see any connection between —" (72). Here Hightower articulates and gives prominence to the text's central narrative instability. Indeed, finding connections between the cause of the fire and Lena is what the remainder of the chapter — and, in some sense, the remainder of the novel — asks the reader to undertake.

Byron, for his part, so orders his narrative as to keep this question tantalizingly open. Each item of data that he offers Hightower, and the reader, is accompanied by a statement that hints at a much more significant piece of information that remains as yet unrevealed. Near the beginning of the chapter, for example, he notes that "I never even suspicioned then that what I didn't know was not the worst of it" (72); and later, "I didn't know myself, then, the other. The rest of it. The worst of it" (75). Suspense is further maintained by his persistent withholding of full disclosure: for a good deal of the chapter, rather than explain "the other," "the rest of it," Byron tells Lena's story (her arrival in town, meeting with Mrs. Beard, etc.). Yet, all the while, the reader is kept aware that there is another, more crucial story that has yet to emerge: Byron notes that Brown was "telling *it*" (80, my emphasis); the boarders at Mrs. Beard's might start "talking about *it*" (81, my emphasis). Reduced to a pronoun, untold, constantly alluded to, this pivotal narrative remains undefined but ubiquitous.

The seriousness and magnitude of this withheld information are further stressed by Byron's proleptic projections of the emotional effects of its full disclosure: as Hightower learns of the first, fairly innocuous detail, that Lena's husband is a bootlegger, "Byron can see in the other's face something latent, about to wake, of which Hightower himself is unaware, as if something inside the man were trying to warn or prepare him" (74). It appears that even the imperturbable Lena "felt foreboding too" when she asked Byron: "What is it them men were trying to tell you? What is it about that burned house?" (77).

Here everything points the reader toward the narrative that concerns "that burned house." It commands present attention and appears absolutely crucial to future development. Faulkner initially called this novel "Dark House,"[19] and the text's controlling mystery seems now to hinge upon the discovery of exactly what caused its "lighting." Each of the characters introduced so far – Lena, Brown, Christmas, Byron, Joanna Burden, and Hightower – seems to have some involvement with it, as does a good deal of the expository detail (the town's attitude toward Joanna, etc.) whose narrative relevance is not yet clear. More importantly, the resolution of the central dynamic plot – Lena's search for her lover – is now directly linked with and subsumed into the process of this disclosure. The revelation of "the worst of it," Byron's understanding of the events that transpired at the Burden house, is revealed immediately after and seemingly as an addition to the detailed reiteration of Lena's arrival at the mill, meeting with Byron, and so on. Lena's story, in fact, is offered to Hightower to explain, in part, the "connection between" the "house that burned yesterday" and "what she had come all the way from Alabama to find" (72). Hightower here receives completely and straightforwardly what the reader has had to pick up piecemeal in chapter 2 – what in this retelling clearly constitutes a continually developing comic plot, a romantic triangle consisting of (1) a pregnant woman, (2) her newly discovered lover (Byron), and (3) the estranged, indifferent father of her child, who seems to be involved in illegal activities connected with the Burden fire. In this recapitulation, moreover, even Hightower has a conventional comic role to play: "Is he still enough of a preacher to marry folks?" Lena asks Byron (82).

Up to this point in the text, the reader is still able, and indeed rhetorically invited, to postulate some horizon of expectations based on the newly complicated but still dominant comic plot that will presumably draw the previous narrative materials together. Although the already prominent pattern of construction/deconstruction keeps pulling us away from it, we are asked, and here most strongly, to prepare for such a coordinating plot configuration, one whose synthesizing forces will become operable once the crucially withheld information is disclosed. In this way, it seems, Faulkner is setting up a structure somewhat like that of Dickens's *Bleak House* (1853), another polyphonic, multistranded novel that revolves around a central mystery, deals with orphans and strangers, jumps between present- and past-tense narration, explores distinctions between public and private identity, and, at bottom, raises questions about interrelation and interpretation. In Dickens's text, seemingly disconnected plots and characters remain in a barely stable equilibrium until the final disclosures retrospectively align related elements and bring to light previously unrealized correspondences, parallels, and connections.

Bleak House, J. Hillis Miller has said, "assimilates everything it touches into a system of meaning";[20] *Light in August,* however, goes only so far in this direction. It pushes the reader toward a system of meaning, but then questions, subverts, and finally, unlike *Bleak House,* deconstructs it, replacing it with another system – only then to repeat the process once again. This complex rhetorical strategy is what gives *Light in August* its formal distinctiveness and peculiar power, distinguishing its organization from that of Faulkner's other narratively discontinuous, polyphonic works. For example, by a corresponding point in the narrative development of *The Wild Palms,* the reader is well aware that the autonomous, alternating narratives will never occupy the same time and space and therefore can never be connected in terms of plot. Similarly, though not so obviously, by the fourth chapter of *Go Down, Moses* we discover that only some characters, some settings, and some time periods are coordinated; again, there is manifestly not enough common ground to link them narratively. In both *The Wild Palms* and *Go Down, Moses* the distinct narrative units must be integrated thematically. Though initially broken and discontinuous like these other texts, *Light in August* – unlike them but more like *Bleak House* – fitfully moves toward, and stimulates the desire for, the establishment of a synthesizing, coordinating line of action. Yet this movement ultimately reaches neither an integrated theme nor an articulated plot, but stresses rather their meaningful dispersions, attempted reconvergences, and final subversions.

It is here, in the middle of chapter 4, that *Light in August*'s comic plot reaches its point of maximum coordinating ability and the drive toward potential interrelation of the narrative materials is at its strongest. But it is here too that Faulkner finally discloses the withheld information that totally confounds and deranges the plot, dislocates narrative expectation, and halts forward progress. Lena's story, as previous hints have warned us, is not all there is; and, at this point, when narrative expectations have reached a climax, Hightower speaks as much for the reader as for himself when he asks: "What is this you are telling me?" And Byron, for his part, responds as much to the reader as to the minister, "with an expression of commiseration and pity. 'I knowed you had not heard yet. I knowed it would be for me to tell you'" (82).

At first, he tells very little; he only offers a few unconnected phrases: "About Christmas. About yesterday and Christmas. Christmas is part nigger. About him and Brown and yesterday" (83). Yet, the story is all here: embedded in these cryptic statements is the seed of an entirely new plot (initially a mystery), a new reading strategy (oriented toward disclosure), and an undoing and retrospective reformulation of what has come before – "I knowed you had not heard." Narrative expectations will revolve around who Christmas is ("About Christmas"), what he has done ("About yesterday and Christmas"), and his interactions with others ("About him and Brown and yesterday"). Most importantly, though, they will circle and recircle around the information that "Christmas is part nigger" (the one full sentence in the group), the ramifications of which come to dominate, disturb, and ultimately deform the text in the same way as do such equally crucial statements as "[Eunice] *Drownd herself*" in *Go Down, Moses* or the even more similar "[Charles Bon's] *mother was part negro*" in *Absalom, Absalom!*.[21]

After this fragmented prelude, we are finally offered the details of the critically withheld story (83–93). But since the novel, as the reader is coming to learn, seems to deal as much with the process of interpretation – the formulation and reformulation of horizons of expectation – as with the interpreted information itself, this disclosure is not offered as a straightforward chronological reconstruction. Byron's narrative not only moves back and forth in time but has embedded within it two other narratives: Brown's story and the deposition of the "countryman" who discovered the fire. Hightower, like the reader, is thus confronted with a mass of new and somewhat confusing materials that cannot be processed in terms of the data at hand.

As we learn about Joanna Burden's murder and the fact that Christmas has been living with her "like man and wife for three years" (86), the explanatory possibilities of Lena's narrative get pushed further and further into the background. By the time we reach the final disclosure, that Christmas has "got nigger blood in him" – a disclosure that Brown, like the text itself, "had been saving . . . for just such a time as this" (90–1) – Lena's plot is virtually impotent: it cannot absorb, explain, or even provide an adequate context for such information. Contrary to what the reader has been led to expect, "the worst of it," "what Byron knows now," turns out to have little to do with the "connection" between Lena and the Burden fire (72); instead, it retrospectively provides a motive for a previously unknown murder plot. The reader, in fact, has been obliged to go through this chapter's frustrating process of gradual disclosure not so that fresh interrelations can be uncovered but so that he or she can – like the community – come to accept (at least provisionally) Christmas's racial identity as the causal explanation for the crime.

The emphatic revelation of Christmas's (as yet unquestioned) black blood changes everything that has come before; even the new mystery plot requires a readjustment of narrative expectations. The question of murder now becomes subordinate to that of race and identity; the marshal warns Brown: "You better be careful what you are saying, if it is a white man you are talking about. . . . I dont care if he is a murderer or not" (91). The town is now confronted with a more heinous crime, a crime of greater sociological and historical profundity, one that affects the racial identities and collective fantasies of an entire people: the rape and murder of a white woman by a reputed black man. It is, indeed, no longer a straightforward felony but a ritualized, mythic act: "an anonymous negro crime committed not by a negro but by Negro" (271).

Although the chapter ends with Lena and the fact that Byron has not yet told her about Brown's attempt to catch Christmas for the reward, the reader soon realizes that any attempt to join Christmas and Lena in the same plot will be confounded. Throughout the first four chapters, the text projects a dynamic set of expectations that keeps the potentiality for the establishment of a centripetal, concerted action just beyond the reader's horizon; when that horizon is finally reached, however, the capping detail opens up a new set of expectations and propels a centrifugal movement away from the expository and narrative materials supplied at an earlier stage. Christmas is specifically introduced into the narrative as a piece that will not fit the developing pattern. Indeed, as the rest of the text goes to show, Christmas is a piece from an altogether different puzzle, and, beginning with chapter 5, the reader is forced to disassemble the previous pattern and start anew.

The possibility that the rhetorical stress on Christmas and the introduction of his story is just another gap or delay in the earlier plot is quickly put to rest: the next seven chapters focus exclusively on him; Lena, Hightower, Byron, and any narrative expectations devolving from them are left aside for the next 180 pages. Christmas's new narrative prominence becomes the text's impasse; it blocks further passage, calls for a rebeginning, and deconstructs prior narrative expectations. It forces the novel to become not a *Bleak House*, where all the initially disparate elements ultimately reach a certain stability, but rather a *Dark House*, where an inexplicable black center disturbingly remains (as in

Absalom, Absalom!, the other novel Faulkner originally called "Dark House"),[22] only to be somewhat "lighted" by competing pressures.

Christmas, as almost all critics have pointed out, is radically divided; he is existentially and psychologically split, torn apart by his unknown racial origins, Calvinist upbringing, and ambivalent attitudes toward woman, sex, time, and his own identity. He cannot locate any stable center around which to perceive or define himself. Yet he is trapped within his torn being; he remains "inside the circle," as he retrospectively realizes: "I have never got outside that circle. I have never broken out of the ring of what I have already done and cannot ever undo" (321). His narrative is similarly split and determined, and the interpretive procedures it progressively compels the reader to experience are directly reflective of this kind of obsessively repeated self-division.

The murder mystery that supplanted the romantic comedy in chapter 4 is Christmas's mystery; it defines him publicly and privately and grows out of everything he has experienced. Coming to terms with Christmas's self-constituting act requires the reader to adopt a new reading strategy. We must put aside narrative expectations projected upon future action – explanation by outcome – and become ever more immersed in the disclosure of the past – explanation by origins. Christmas's narrative thus becomes a narrative of ever-receding and ever-proliferating expositions. These attempt to provide what all expositions attempt to provide: "the specific antecedents indispensable" to an understanding of the story. Here, however, the various materials will not come together; the expository data will not coalesce; the antecedents will not explain; everything and nothing is indispensable.

Every time a clarifying narrative begins to emerge, such as the detailed chronological delineation of Christmas's various primal confrontations – racial, sexual, familial, religious – which make up most of chapters 6–12, new and unexpected materials break in and exposition begins anew. For example, as soon as the account of Christmas's past begins to approach the fictive present, his discourse becomes invaded by that of Joanna Burden. Her narrative, which deals entirely with her ancestors (227–40), extends even further into the past and further complicates not only her private relationship with Christmas but the public, religious, and historical dimensions of that relationship: "The curse of every white child that ever was born and that ever will be born . . . [T]he black shadow in the shape of a cross" (239). Similarly, after Christmas's capture, present action is again interrupted by the introduction of yet another set of characters (the Hineses) and another large block of expository materials, explaining both their antecedents and their links to Christmas, which takes up a good deal of chapters 15 and 16. These materials, as well, offer a new set of narrative expectations: the murder mystery is replaced by another disclosure plot – the discovery of the orphan's parents ("What did you do with Milly's baby?" [330]) – that powerfully reintroduces the question of Christmas's lack of identity in terms of a fresh series of actions revolving around family and heredity.

Each narrative that attempts to explain Christmas inevitably postulates other narratives, other voices, other pasts, and other plots. Each horizon of expectations offers further horizons that must take into account new characters, actions, and ways of interpreting. The reader learns, through this rhetorical conditioning, that Christmas's contradictory being cannot be rendered as narrative. Like his life, his story cannot come together. His discourse remains polyphonic and his fundamentally inexplicable identity becomes reflected in a dynamic and problematic process of anti-narrative.

Even at the climax of his story, when he is making his final bid for freedom, the narrative is again disrupted. The action is halted, a new character – Percy Grimm – is introduced, fresh expository information is offered, and previously unexplored political concerns come to the fore. Through this process of interruption and deflection, the fundamental indeterminacy of Christmas's identity becomes duplicated in the reading experience itself. Christmas, like his narrative, cannot achieve closure, and the final description of his mutilated body is presented in terms not of termination or cessation but of continuation and perpetuity:

> [F]rom out the slashed garments about his hips and loins the pent black blood seemed to rush like a released breath. It seemed to rush out of his pale body like the rush of sparks from a rising rocket; upon that black blast the man seemed to rise soaring into their

memories forever and ever. They are not to lose it, in whatever peaceful valleys, beside whatever placid and reassuring streams of old age, in the mirroring faces of whatever children they will contemplate old disasters and newer hopes. It will be there, musing, quiet, steadfast, not fading and not particularly threatful, but of itself alone serene, of itself alone triumphant. (p. 440)

That "it," moreover, remains haunting, problematic, and unfinished is indicated by the inability of the narrative proliferation to stop as well. Even after the reader knows of Christmas's death, another new character – Gavin Stevens, "the District Attorney, a Harvard graduate" (419) – is introduced and allowed to postulate yet another explanatory narrative: "I think I know why it was, why he . . ." (421). Yet Stevens, like the reader, can never come to "know why it was"; the myriad pressures – racial, social, religious, sexual, temporal, political, familial – that keep Christmas self-divided and "other," outside the realm of human love and relationship, remain necessarily and disturbingly destabilized.

As we have seen, the reader's progressive movement through the text is destabilized as well. From the very beginning of the novel, Faulkner has so organized the text as to keep the reading experience centrifugal, multiple, and – in the fullest sense of the term – polyphonic. The centripetal pull toward stability and control is continually countered and undermined by techniques that force the reader to experience and respond to the plurality of the autonomous characters' voices, modes of behavior, and patterns of action. The undercutting of Lena's narrative and the impossibility of Christmas's serve to keep both of them open, not globally integrated, but sustained in a kind of discontinuous dialogue. Each moves in its own direction, sometimes with, sometimes against the other. But each keeps the other from gaining the commanding position, so that although they may briefly intersect, they can never truly connect. This is perhaps most clearly seen in the textual crossings that occur after chapter 13, when Lena's narrative has become prominent once again. When, for example, Mrs. Hines mistakes Lena's newly born child for her own lost grandson – Christmas – or when Lena further compounds this confusion by imagining that Christmas is the child's father (376, 387–8, 422–3), the orphan plot (the search for Milly's baby) touches for a moment Lena's plot (the search for another baby's estranged father). Yet what is emphasized is how one line of action passes the other, not how they meet. No encompassing horizon of expectations can be built from the crossing; after the momentary interaction reopens the central questions of race and identity, the two narrative lines go their separate ways.

This insistent "dialogizing" of the narrative, to use Bakhtin's term, and the process by which the reader is forced constantly to attend to its tensions, continue to the text's very end. As the three opening chapters chronicled Lena's, Hightower's, and Christmas's arrivals in Jefferson, so the three final chapters deal with what are, in a sense, their departures. More importantly, just as the opening three initially undermined the possibility of formal unity by their separate expositions, so the discontinuities of the last three work to confirm and finalize the overriding narrative indeterminacy.

In chapters 19, 20, and 21, the reader is presented with three rhetorically distinct narrative terminations, none of which even attempts to bring the novel into a stable unity. Indeed, these chapters flaunt their disconnectedness; rather than coordinate the text's antecedents, they bring to the fore new characters (Percy Grimm, Cinthy, the furniture repairer), new exposition (Grimm's past, Hightower's youth, his grandfather's exploits), and even new narrative instabilities (the question of Hightower's death, the future for Byron and Lena). All three, moreover, move in every direction except toward the kind of "retrospective patterning" of previous details that projects a stable "sense of ending":[23] the final image of chapter 19 soars upward and out of the narrative in a horrific apotheosis of Christmas's indeterminate identity; chapter 20 travels ever backward beyond the materials of the text toward Hightower's fantasized origins; and chapter 21 propels the fictive present away from Yoknapatawpha County and its concerns as Lena and Byron move out of the town and toward an undisclosed but certainly imaginable future.

At the book's close, then, Faulkner rhetorically heightens the reader's experience of the wholly dialogical and thus indeterminate nature of the text's ordering of materials. The different narratives cannot come together but can only keep each other, as it were, in line; through a carefully orchestrated process of mutual subversion and deconstruction, the reader repeatedly experiences new and unstable horizons of expectation and, more importantly, the vanishing points of those horizons. *Light in August* thus keeps both the individual narrative voices and the silences between those voices inexhaustibly present. It is this kind of truly polyphonic structure that Bakhtin sees as the special province and ultimate goal of the novel as a genre. And it may have been this structure as well that prompted Faulkner himself to distinguish *Light in August* from his other works by proudly asserting on its completion: "This one is a novel: not an anecdote."[24]

NOTES

1. *Selected Letters of William Faulkner,* ed. Joseph Blotner (New York: Random House, 1977), p. 66.

2. Mikhail Bakhtin, *Problems of Dostoevsky's Poetics,* ed. and trans. Caryl Emerson (Minneapolis: University of Minnesota Press, 1984), esp. pp. 6–7, 40.

3. Frederick L. Gwynn and Joseph L. Blotner, eds. *Faulkner in the University: Class Conferences at the University of Virginia, 1957–1958* (Charlottesville: University of Virginia Press, 1959), pp. 8, 122; James B. Meriwether and Michael Millgate, eds., *Lion in the Garden: Interviews with William Faulkner 1926–1962* (New York: Random House, 1968), p. 244.

4. Gwynn and Blotner, eds., *Faulkner in the University,* p. 45.

5. Regina K. Fadiman, *Faulkner's "Light in August": A Description and Interpretation of the Revisions* (Charlottesville: University Press of Virginia, 1975).

6. Roland Barthes, *S/Z,* trans. Richard Miller (New York: Hill & Wang, 1974), pp. 17–21.

7. See, for example, Wolfgang Iser, *The Act of Reading: A Theory of Aesthetic Response* (Baltimore: Johns Hopkins University Press, 1978), pp. 107–18.

8. Meir Sternberg, *Expositional Modes and Temporal Ordering in Fiction* (Baltimore: Johns Hopkins University Press, 1978), pp. 93–8.

9. William Faulkner, "An Introduction for *The Sound and the Fury,*" ed. James B. Meriwether, *Southern Review* n.s. 8 (Autumn 1972):709.

10. François L. Pitavy, Introduction to *William Faulkner's "Light in August": A Critical Casebook* (New York: Garland, 1982), pp. ix–xviii.
11. Cleanth Brooks, *William Faulkner: The Yoknapatawpha Country* (New Haven, Conn.: Yale University Press, 1963), p. 54.
12. Martin Kreiswirth, "Centers, Openings, and Endings: Some Faulknerian Constants," *American Literature* 56 (March 1984):38–50.
13. Sternberg, *Expositional Modes*, p. 1.
14. Ibid., pp. 23–34.
15. Austin Wright, *The Formal Principle in the Novel* (Ithaca, N.Y.: Cornell University Press, 1982), p. 127.
16. Roman Ingarden, *The Literary Work of Art: An Investigation on the Borderlines of Ontology, Logic, and Theory of Literature,* trans. George G. Grabowicz (Evanston, Ill.: Northwestern University Press, 1973), chap. 3.
17. Wright, *Formal Principle,* p. 127.
18. Gerald Prince, "Introduction to the Study of the Narratee," in *Reader-Response Criticism: From Formalism to Post-Structuralism,* ed. Jane P. Tompkins (Baltimore: Johns Hopkins University Press, 1980), pp. 7–25.
19. Fadiman, *Faulkner's "Light in August,"* p. 9.
20. J. Hillis Miller, Introduction to *Bleak House,* by Charles Dickens (Harmondsworth: Penguin, 1971), p. 29.
21. William Faulkner, *Go Down, Moses* (1942; reprint New York: Vintage Books, 1973), p. 267; *Absalom, Absalom!* (1936; reprint New York: Vintage Books, 1972), p. 355.
22. Blotner, ed., *Selected Letters,* p. 78.
23. Barbara Herrnstein Smith, *Poetic Closure: A Study of How Poems End* (Chicago: University of Chicago Press, 1968), pp. 10–14.
24. Blotner, ed., *Selected Letters,* p. 66.

Light in August: The Closed Society and Its Subjects

ANDRÉ BLEIKASTEN

Until the subject of a tyrant's will
Became, worse fate, the abject of his own
— Percy Bysshe Shelley, *Prometheus Unbound*

A S has often been pointed out, none of the main characters of *Light in August* belongs to the community of Jefferson.[1] They are all outsiders, if not outcasts, living in isolation, and in sharp contrast to most of Faulkner's earlier and later books, the family here fails to serve its purpose as mediating agency between individual and society.

"The Community and the Pariah," the title of Cleanth Brooks's classic study of the novel, aptly summarizes its central theme.[2] And Brooks is equally right to call attention to the specific nature of the social environment in which the destinies of its characters are acted out: a traditional rural society, such as could still be found in the Deep South of the twenties and thirties — a society or, to use Brooks's term, a "community," a tightly knit social organization with something like an "organic" character, whose stability is guaranteed by unanimous acceptance of inherited values and unquestioning compliance with established cultural codes. Brooks, however, is not content with underscoring the community's pull and power; he celebrates it as a "positive norm,"[3] the ideal standard by which all individual actions ought to be judged. The causes of Joe Christmas's or Joanna Burden's sufferings are then not far to seek: if both lead miserable lives and die violent deaths, it is essentially because, in departing from the social roles prescribed for them, they have forfeited their right to membership in the community. Conversely, if both Hightower and Byron

81

Bunch are eventually "redeemed," it is because they have found their way back into the communal fold. In his reading of the novel Brooks refers several times to the characters' state of "alienation," but he never seriously considers the possibility that alienation might originate, at least partially, in some flaw of the social fabric itself. To him the outsiders and outcasts of *Light in August* are primarily deviants, and his assumptions about deviance are those that have been held by conservative social thinkers from Plato to Parsons: deviance proceeds from *anomie*, that is, lawlessness, a lack of temperance and restraint, a collapse of personal morality.[4] Which is to say that, whatever the circumstances may be, conformity is right, rebellion wrong; in the last resort, the wretched of the earth have only themselves to blame for their wretchedness.

There is little in *Light in August*, however, to warrant such a reading. Admittedly, one can find decent people in Jefferson as everywhere, and not all outsiders are brutally rejected by the community. Thus, even though Lena Grove has transgressed its sexual code, everybody takes her in and treats her with kindness. But the benevolence accorded to the pregnant girl should not make one forget Hightower's beating up by the KKK or Christmas's murder and mutilation by Percy Grimm. Extremist groups like the KKK and fanatics like Grimm may not be typical; still, they do the community's dirty work, and act as the unofficial agents of collective violence. Technically, the assassination of Christmas is perhaps no "lynching,"[5] but it is condoned beforehand by the mob hysteria that sets in as soon as it is rumored that a white woman has been murdered.[6] The community, then, to put it mildly, cannot be exonerated of all guilt. Even if it seems to disavow its self-appointed defenders and avengers, it supports their misdeeds by its cowardice and sanctions them by its consenting silence.

In *Light in August*, as in most of Faulkner's novels, the individual and the collective are inextricably entangled. Like all great novelists, Faulkner was well aware that individuality and society were always locked in a relationship of reciprocity: no one, not even the outsider, is outside the jurisdiction of society; we are all within society, for no sooner are we born than society is within us and starts to pattern our lives.

Whenever a conflict arises, it is therefore bound to become a war on two fronts: the enemy is both without and within. Christmas's destiny is a case in point. The conflict he is engaged in is at once an open contest with the community and a psychomachia, a long, fierce struggle of self against self, and it is one of the novel's supreme ironies that the origin of this dual conflict lies not at all in actual race difference but in fantasies – both public and private – about race. Christmas is not a black man pitted against the white community; he probably is not even a mulatto. There is no factual evidence for his mixed blood: his being partly black is sheer conjecture, and it should be remembered that the first person to conceive the hypothesis and to convert it into a certainty is Doc Hines, the rabid racist who happens to be Christmas's grandfather.[7] Christmas's cruel secret is the unresolved riddle of his birth. His is, according to Faulkner himself, "the most tragic condition a man could find himself in – not to know what he is and to know that he will never know."[8] He does not know, but he often thinks he knows; he believes because he has been made to believe.[9] As a child, at the Memphis orphanage, he became aware of himself as an object of contempt and hatred through the other children's taunting voices, through the dietitian's invectives, and above all through Hines's watchful gaze.[10] Under more favorable circumstances, discovering himself to be different might have been a normal stage in the individuation process, perhaps even a positive step toward autonomy; for Christmas, though, it marked the beginning of his schizoid sense of himself as self-estranged and heralded a future of isolation, alienation, and fragmentation. And once the judgment passed upon him by hostile others had been internalized, he would never stop loathing himself, consumed both by the white racist's hatred of the "nigger" and the black man's hatred of his white oppressor.

To have an identity: to be one; to have two identities: to be no one. Christmas is a walking oxymoron and its negation: both white and black, and *neither*. He might choose, he could "pass," yet he chooses not to choose, refuses to settle for either of the ready-made identity patterns urged upon him by Southern society. Were he able to merge or transcend them, he could achieve a self beyond race truly his own, but the feat cannot be accomplished and the dice are loaded anyway. So all he can do is to cling to his refusal, to persevere in his no-saying, to affirm what is left of his humanity through repudiation and revolt.[11]

In delving into the depths of Christmas's memory Faulkner enables the reader to trace his tragedy back to its origin in childhood and youth. *Light in August,* however, though largely focused on the ravages of racism in an individual psyche, does not leave its public dimension out of account. Christmas's journey into darkness starts in an orphanage under the petrifying stare of a paranoid grandfather; when it reaches its final stage, there is once again an evil eye, but this time it is a collective one: the "organ" of the lynch mob gathered around Joanna's burning house.[12] Between the "ordinary" racism of the white community, most often latent but easily reactivated in times of tension, and the virulent, never abating racism of men like Hines or Grimm, the difference is at best one of degree, and little is needed to cancel the difference. Racism in Jefferson is a chronic and endemic disease, to the contagion of which no one, whether white or black, is totally immune.

Yet, just as Christmas's split self has been generated by an old man's manic suspicion, racism rests on nothing but preconceptions and misconceptions, and draws its power from a shared fiction. In the course of his erratic career Christmas is victimized by various people, but all of his victimizers pay allegiance to the same myths, and Christmas, the victim, is himself trapped within them. It could hardly be otherwise: his standards are all white standards, the only ones that have ever been available to him. Race hatred was instilled in him by his grandfather; McEachern, his foster father, taught him the harsh virtues of white Protestant virility and a solid contempt for women. Their teaching has made him what he is: a racist, a sexist, and a Puritan. Mentally and emotionally, he is indeed a white Southern male – or would be, did he not believe himself to be tainted with blackness.

What makes Christmas's position untenable is that he feels simultaneously imprisoned in and excluded from his white fathers' value system. However stubborn his desire to refuse, however heroic his will to resist, his entire being is caught in the social machinery, and at the end, inexorably, as in Kafka's *Penal Colony,* the death sentence will be inscribed on the prisoner's flesh. As Christmas himself comes to realize toward the close of his desperate search/flight, he has never been able to break out of the "circle" of his predetermined fate, and even his death is a false exit, since his crime – the slaying of a white woman – and its punishment – his being killed and castrated – provide the long awaited opportunity to coerce him into a recognizable identity and make him play a repertoried role. In death, as scapegoat, Christmas has at last become of service to the community. And, through the sacrificial magic of atonement, he has at last become *one*.

It is through the very paradox of his predicament that Christmas develops in the novel into a highly emblematic figure. Not that he is in any way typical in social or ethnic terms. But his eccentricity takes us to the very core of the Southern experience. Christmas is anything but representative of the South, yet in his single and singular fate he embodies its ambiguities and contradictions, acts out its conflicts, exemplifies in almost allegorical fashion the principle of division that both holds it together and threatens to tear it apart.

In much the same way Joanna Burden, for all her ties with the North, is used to explore some of the hidden recesses of the Southern mind.[13] Besides, Joe and Joanna, already twinned by their first names, are very much alike. Joe has known neither of his parents and Joanna bows under the "burden" of a family tradition, but they share an abiding obsession with race, transmitted to them at a very early age and closely associated for both with the indelible memory of a father and/or a grandfather. These figures are, in turn, surprisingly similar. Though alleged to be from New England, Joanna's grandfather Calvin is in his theological fanaticism a worthy match for Doc Hines: both regard the black man as the accursed of God; the abolitionist's militant Negrophilia and the white supremacist's demented Negrophobia are antithetical rationalizations of the same racist delirium. Furthermore, if Joe's father, according to rumor, might have been a Mexican, Joanna has been named after Juana, her father's first Mexican wife, who looked exactly like Evangeline, her father's French Huguenot mother. In the chronicle of the Burdens, as recounted by Joanna to Joe, these women and their progeny are evoked as if they belonged to another race, and the physical contrast between Calvin and his son Nathaniel is heavily emphasized: "the tall, gaunt,

Nordic man, and the small, dark, vivid child who had inherited his mother's build and coloring, like people of two different races" (229). Even more revealing are Calvin's outraged remarks when he sees Juana's son for the first time: " 'Another damn black Burden,' he said. 'Folks will think I bred to a damn slaver. And now he's got to breed to one too' . . . 'Damn, lowbuilt black folks: low built because of the weight of the wrath of God, black because of the sin of human bondage staining their blood and flesh" (234). Prurient Puritans, the male Burdens were obviously attracted to "dark" ladies and beset with the exotic sin of miscegenation. No wonder then that Joanna, their female descendant, should repeat the pattern in reverse in becoming the mistress of a man whom she believes to be a mulatto and who may remind her – incestuously? – of her half-brother, shot at the age of twenty "over a question of negro voting" (235).

Like Joe's, Joanna's initiation into evil took place in early childhood. She was (re)born into guilt on the day her father took her to the grave of her grandfather and her half-brother to invest her with the curse of the white race:

> "Remember this. Your grandfather and brother are lying there, murdered not by one white man but by the curse which God put on a whole race before your grandfather or your brother or me or you were even thought of. A race doomed and cursed to be forever and ever a part of the white race's doom and curse for its sins. Remember that. His doom and his curse. Forever and ever. Mine. Your mother's. Yours, even though you are a child. The curse of every white child that ever was born and that ever will be born. None can escape it." (p. 239)

Words inflict wounds. Both testament and prophecy, the paternal pronouncement marks Joanna forever. There could hardly be a better illustration of the performative power of language. The father's words have conjured up a world of division and guilt, and for Joanna their magic is to last to the very end; their evil enchantment will never be dispelled:

> "I had seen and known negroes since I could remember. I just looked at them as I did at rain, or furniture, or food or sleep. But after that I seemed to see them for the first time not as people, but as a thing, a shadow in which I lived, we lived, all white people, all

86

other people. I thought of all the children coming forever and ever into the world, white, with the black shadow already falling upon them before they drew breath. And I seemed to see the black shadow in the shape of a cross. And it seemed like the white babies were struggling, even before they drew breath, to escape from the shadow that was not only upon them but beneath them too, flung out like their arms were flung out, as if they were nailed to the cross. I saw all the little babies that would ever be in the world, the ones not yet even born − a long line of them with their arms spread, on the black crosses." (p. 239)

The father's *speech* is followed immediately by the daughter's bleak *vision* of universal and endless agony. But, ironically enough, the crucified child is first of all Joanna herself, nailed by her own father on the cross of a triple identity, a triple filiation. Through the baptismal rite on the ancestral grave she has entered simultaneously the family line, the white Southern community, and the communion of the damned, her fate sealed once and for all by the decree of three blended voices: the actual, living voice of her father, the posthumous voice of her grandfather, and, lending absolute authority to both, the remote overvoice of the heavenly Father.

With Faulkner, the Father − especially the Dead Father − is always the one who names, places, marks, the one who casts the spell, whether through his voice or his eyes.[14] Like so many of Faulkner's doomed characters, both Joanna and Joe testify in their ultimate helplessness to the Father's irresistible power, and the identity impressed upon the former is hardly more viable than the latter's nonidentity: fractured and fraught with guilt from the start, marked out for suffering and disaster. Joanna will never escape from the "black shadow," nor will Joe ever cease to perceive himself through the hate-filled eyes of a white. There is nothing metaphysical or theological about Faulknerian predestination: it is all a matter of evil utterances and evil eyes, of human, all too human predictions and previsions.

Joe's and Joanna's encounter is the fortuitous but fatal collision of two lives under the same malediction, their affair the inevitable working out of two complementary designs. By the end of their stormy relationship Joe has become for Joanna the "shadow" and the "cross"; for Joe, Joanna ends up as an ominous reincarnation of his first persecutor, "cold, dead white, fanatical, mad" (262). The time is ripe then for their final confrontation; the process of mutual destruction is now to come to its predictable end. When Joanna, recalling her father's speech and identifying with her fathers' will, insists on confining Joe within his mythic "Negro" identity, Joe has no other course but to kill her.

Even in the earlier "sewer" phase, however, Joanna in "the wild throes of nymphomania" would call him "Negro! Negro! Negro!" (245). Race and sex are at stake in the liaison from first to last, and they appear as correlate issues throughout the narrative of Christmas's life and death. Again. *cherchez l'enfant:* "You little nigger bastard!" (114), the dietitian hisses in fury, dragging the five-year-old boy from behind the curtain where he had hidden to eat her toothpaste while she was making love with a young doctor. The toothpaste episode is the "primal scene" in the course of which Joe's sense of blackness gets enmeshed for the first time with the temptations and terrors of sex. Henceforth womanhood, food, and sexuality will be joined with his racial obsession in a single knot of guilt.[15] A pattern has been set for Joe's whole sexual career: of his successive encounters with women, from his failed initiation with a young black prostitute through his affair with Bobbie to his involvement with Joanna, there is scarcely one that does not end in similar fashion with extreme bewilderment and violent repudiation. As an adult, Joe cannot make love to a white woman without telling her about his black blood, and the idea of a white woman consenting to sleep with a black man is as unbearable to him as to any white racist. It takes two policemen to prevent him from killing a white prostitute for her indifference to his blackness, and her attitude upsets him so deeply that after the incident he stays "sick" for two years (212). Conversely, having chosen to live "as man and wife with a woman who resembled an ebony carving," he is unable to share her bed without "his whole being [writhing] and [straining] with physical outrage and spiritual denial" (212). At each encounter, sexual difference is exacerbated by (presumed) racial difference. Always the antagonist, Joe feels black with a white woman and white with a black one. Sexual intercourse is to him twice cursed and twice tabooed, and so experienced each time as a monstrous mating, a kind of reciprocal rape bound to end in either nausea or murderous fury.

In Yoknapatawpha County sexism and racism go hand in hand. Luminous Lena notwithstanding, Woman and "Negro" alike appear throughout most of *Light in August* as carriers of strangeness and disorder, as uncanny, menacing figures of radical *otherness*, and they appear as such not only to the white male characters in the novel, but also, albeit much more ambiguously, to the reader. Even though Christmas's story is enclosed by the bright circle of Lena's journey, *Light in August* is indeed a tale of "darkness,"[16] and its haunting rhetoric of corruption, with its Hawthornian dark/light imagery and its rich array of liquid metaphors (pools, pits, sewers, swamps, morasses), invariably refers back to the *other race* and/or the *other sex*, and suggests over and over again the disquieting closeness of an abysmal blackness in which both are secret sharers. The supreme horror, the ultimate abomination, is therefore the "womanshenegro" (147): blackness at its thickest and foulest, blackness with a vengeance.

Nowhere in the novel is this fantasmal equivalence of femininity and negritude as flagrant as in the scene at Freedman Town recounted at the end of chapter 5, just before the long retrospective sequence opening in the next chapter. Christmas's nocturnal visit to the Negro section of Jefferson is his descent into hell, an apposite *mise en abîme* of his whole life as well as a prefiguration of his imminent death:

> As from the bottom of a thick black pit he saw himself enclosed by cabinshapes . . . as if the black life, the black breathing had compounded the substance of breath so that not only voices but moving bodies and light itself must become fluid and accrete slowly from particle to particle, of and with the now ponderable night inseparable and one. (p. 107)

Darkness here has conquered everything and everybody. Even light has been absorbed into the opaque and fluid substance of the night, and for Christmas the night, filled with "the bodiless fecundmellow voices of negro women" (107), soon turns into a nightmare, the nightmare of "the lightless hot wet primogenitive

Female" (107), which threatens to engulf his precarious manhood.

Christmas then runs up the hill, "out of the black hollow" to "the cold hard air of white people" (107). Yet the dark pit from which he flees in revulsion and terror, as if it were "the original quarry, abyss itself" (108), is described as a place of teeming fertility, and the voices he hears there are the mellow murmuring voices of primal motherhood. But to Christmas the (m)other's tongue is an alien idiom, "a language not his" (107), which he cannot and will not understand and listen to, because it speaks the unspeakable, the "other" without a name.[17] Like all male characters in the novel, Christmas fears and hates the raw powers of life embodied by the "primogenitive Female": life is bearable only to the extent that it is "manshaped" (107).

Life at its enigmatic source is disorderly, random, unpredictable. Hence the male strategies of containment, division, and control and the establishment of a repressive, male-made, and male-centered social order founded on the subjection of women to men and blacks to whites. Hence also the need for an ideology – or, if you prefer, a mythology – capable of investing maleness and whiteness with a measure of legitimacy. In *Light in August* the most vociferous spokesman of racist and sexist ideology is Doc Hines, yet nearly everybody subscribes to its basic tenets: only the white man can claim the priveleges of full and soverign humanity; he alone is entitled to lay down the Law. Women and blacks, on the other hand, the dangerous representatives of that which exceeds and negates all representation, are assigned to an inferior essence, and so are quite "naturally" destined to occupy subordinate positions in the social structure.

Such is the dominant discourse, and Faulkner allows us to measure its effects, to see how it works, how it warps, and how it kills. Count the corpses: Milly Hines bled to death by her own father, Hightower's wife driven to suicide, Joanna slain and beheaded, Christmas shot and emasculated – three women and one "nigger." Their tragic deaths are eloquent testimony to the murderous violence of Southern ideology; yet, as we have already seen, its everyday ravages, though less visible and more insidious, are no less appalling: crippled minds, split selves, destruction from with-

90

in. Christmas is no doubt the most exemplary case of self-division and self-laceration, but just as he wavers between his racial identities, so Joanna switches back and forth between her sexual identities. At the beginning of their affair, Christmas is impressed by, perhaps even secretly attracted to, her "mantrained muscles" (221), her "mantrained habit of thinking" (221–2), and deeply perplexed by the "almost manlike yielding of [her] surrender" (221). Even more stubbornly than she resists her outside aggressor, Joanna resists her own femininity, denying her flesh and sex in the very act of surrender, inviolate in violation, evincing that "imperviousness" to experience and change that in Faulkner's fiction is generally the index of masculine "innocence." Even in her second "phase," when succumbing to the filth and fury of seemingly naked lust, her "dual personality" (221) persists, for what she then seeks is not so much erotic gratification as the final, inexpiable transgression of the twofold – racial and sexual – taboo, which will ensure her damnation. Her mind keeps hovering above the obscene spectacle of the sinning flesh like a horrified voyeur, her body being no more acknowledged as *her own* in debauchery than it was in chastity.[18]

Joanna is at war with her womanhood as Christmas is with his blackness. For neither can there be acceptance of otherness within self. Subjection or abjection is the only alternative.

Masculine standards, white standards: tracing identical boundaries, serving identical purposes, they are the pillars of the power system, known as the Law, which governs the community and to which every one of its members is summoned to submit. And woe to the offenders: sooner or later they will be dismembered – not only ostracized but broken apart, body and soul.

For once, the hackneyed phrase "dominant ideology" seems perfectly appropriate. Southern ideology, however, has yet another, more official component: *Puritanism*,[19] ideological discourse at its most articulate and most intimidating, the common idiom by means of which the community defines and vindicates its priorities, and whose authority is the more undisputed as it is assumed to be derived from divine transcendence itself. Indeed, whenever racist or sexist prejudice is spelled out, as it is by Doc

91

Hines, McEachern, and Joanna's father and grandfather, the rhetoric assumes at once the harshly prophetic accents of Old Testament eloquence, and the final justification for any belief or behavior is nearly always theological. The rantings of backwoods fanatics like Hines can, of course, be readily dismissed as crude travesties of true Christianity and even as debased versions of its Calvinistic variant. The point, though, is that no one in Jefferson (with the partial and paradoxical exceptions of Hightower, the renegade Presbyterian minister, and of Byron Bunch, Faulkner's triumphant comic rebel, the only male character not irremediably locked in his cultural conditioning, and therefore capable of learning from experience) is able to express ideas on moral, social, or racial matters outside the framework of ingrained religious concepts. Puritanism imposes itself as an all but exclusive way of thinking and speaking, and insofar as it filters and controls people's thoughts and words, it patterns their very lives, netting them in its rigid code of prescriptions and prohibitions, requiring strict observance of its norms, and calling for ruthless punishment whenever the latter are violated. A collective neurosis as all cultures are, the Puritan culture dramatized in Faulkner's novel originates in and rests upon repression. What sets it apart is that the amount of repression exacted is exceptionally high, the neurosis exceptionally severe. Based on the presumption of humanity's innate depravity, Puritan morality stresses the need to discipline the body and mortify the flesh so as to ward off temptation. Flesh is filth, sex is sin, or, as Hines puts it, "Bitchery and abomination" (341). Life, for the Puritan, can only be life in death and for death, and for Joanna, the martyr of Calvinism, and Christmas, the Puritan *malgré lui*, it is indeed nothing else.

With the exposure and denunciation of Puritanism as life-negating, we are, of course, on fairly familiar ground. *Light in August*, however, goes well beyond the by now commonplace equation of Puritanism with sexual repression. For if it leaves us in no doubt as to the debilitating effects of the Puritan ethos on individuals, it allows us as well to detect the economic uses of repression: it is not simply a matter of subduing bodies in order to save souls; the sexual energies deflected from their natural goals are destined to become socially productive through work.

Simon McEachern, Joe Christmas's Presbyterian foster father, is in this respect the key figure: work is one of the articles of his faith; his is the Protestant work ethic in all its rigor, but also with its typical sense of ownership. In fact, his relations to other persons are all patterned on those of owner to owned. On arriving at the orphanage, he looks at the five-year-old Joe with "the same stare with which he might have examined a horse or a second hand plow" (133) and takes delivery of him as though he were a mere commodity. Once he has adopted him, he treats him like an object to be fashioned at will by its possessor. True, McEachern is also a man of duty, ready to assume responsibility for his possessions, and so pledges himself to take care of the child as he has done so far of his wife, his cattle, and his fields. The adoption, for him, is ruled by a businesslike mutual agreement, and he informs Joe without delay of what he takes to be its terms:

> "You will find food and shelter and the care of Christian people. . . . And the work within your strength that will keep you out of mischief. For I will have you learn soon that the two abominations are sloth and idle thinking, the two virtues are work and the fear of God." (p. 135)

In teaching Joe the Presbyterian catechism, McEachern will do his best — and worst — to beat these virtues into his recalcitrant mind. However, if the boy must be taught the prophylactic virtue of toil, it is equally important for his foster father that he should be given proper training for his future tasks. Joe is his putative son, after all, who some day will inherit his property. Hence the gift of the heifer, a highly pedagogic gesture intended to teach the boy "the responsibility of possessing, owning, ownership" as well as "foresight and aggrandisement" (153). Yet once again McEachern's pedagogy fails: Joe sells the cow to buy himself a new suit. Had he sold it for a profit, McEachern would have forgiven him; what he cannot condone, however, is that Joe has sold it for his pleasure or, more precisely, for "whoring" (154). The sin is the more unpardonable in that it combines waste with lechery. Sexual morality and economic morality are the two sides of the same coin. To McEachern as to all Puritans, gratuitous expenditure and instant sensuous gratification are anathema; work, thrift, the pursuit of profit, and the accumulation of wealth, on the other hand, are approved of as intrinsically virtuous. Renounce the pleasures of the flesh, work hard, and get rich *ad majorem Dei gloriam:* such are the major commandments of McEachern's religion. It owes at least as much to Benjamin Franklin as to Calvin.

Sober manners, stern self-control, coldness in interpersonal relations, devotion to work, thrift, and gain – all these features remind one of the "worldly asceticism" that Max Weber regarded as essential to the rise of capitalism.[20] And in this connection one might also note the many hints in the novel at what Weber called the "religious foundations"[21] of Protestant asceticism. In *Light in August* religious imagery is pervasive, and never so abundant as in the chilling scenes of Joe's indoctrination by McEachern:

> [The boy] was looking straight ahead, with a rapt, calm expression like a monk in a picture. (p. 140)

> Save for surplice he might have been a Catholic choir boy, with for nave the looming and shadowy crib. . . . (p. 140)

> Then he returned to the bed, carrying the empty tray as though it were a monstrance and he the bearer, his surplice the cutdown undergarment which had been bought for a man to wear. (p. 145)

> The boy's body might have been wood or stone; a post or a tower upon which the sentient part of him mused like a hermit, contemplative and remote with ecstasy and selfcrucifixion. (p. 150)

Hieratic postures, sacerdotal garments: it is as if the stark simplicity of the Presbyterian catechesis were given the lie by the ceremonious formality of Catholic liturgy. The immediate purpose of this imagery is no doubt to underscore the disturbing ritualistic quality of McEachern's and Joe's sadomasochistic relationship, yet there are other characters in the novel who are likened to monks and hermits and thus bring to mind the monastic practices of another age. Once again, Faulkner plays on contrasts and continuities, suggests the permanence, across centuries, of cultural traditions, and points to the recurrence of identical types of behavior. Whatever the differences between the mystical asceticism of early Christianity and the secular asceticism of Puritan America, they both bespeak the same compulsive urge to raise mind above matter, soul above flesh, the same monstrous pride in the guise of humility.

Puritan asceticism turns out to be yet another detour and disease of desire. What is repressed returns and takes revenge. Pain changes places with pleasure, and it is in violence, spontaneous or ritualized, individual or collective, that the Puritan seeks the "ecstasy" he is forbidden to experience otherwise:

> Pleasure, ecstasy, they cannot seem to bear: their escape from it is in violence, in drinking and fighting and praying; catastrophe too, the violence identical and apparently inescapable *And so why should not their religion drive them to crucifixion of themselves and one another?* (p. 347)

In Hightower's thoughts — which one would be tempted to suspect if they did not seem to have the narrator's approval[22] — Puritanism is explicitly accused of being the main cause of violence and suffering. Christ's sacrifice on the cross is no longer associated with the glad tidings of redemption: "crucifixion" has become an ironic paradigm of the torments men inflict on themselves and on others.

On Sunday evening, at twilight, sitting once again at his window, Hightower is listening to the music which comes to him from the church where he once used to preach:

> The organ strains come rich and resonant through the summer night, blended, sonorous, with that quality of abjectness and sublimation, as if the freed voices themselves were assuming the shapes and attitudes of crucifixions, ecstatic, solemn, and profound in gathering volume. Yet even then the music has still a quality stern and implacable, deliberate and without passion so much as immolation, pleading, asking, for not love, not life, forbidding it to others, demanding in sonorous tones death as though death were the boon, like all Protestant music. (p. 347)

This is the music we listen to in *Light in August:* a sinister celebration of death inspired by a religion of death. Whether in writing the novel Faulkner intended to indict Christianity or at any rate Protestantism remains debatable. For all we know, he was by no means hostile to Christian religion, and a judicious appraisal of his fictional treatment of religious matters would obviously require a good deal of circumspection and tact. One can hardly fail to be struck, however, by the utter fierceness of the attack in the two passages just quoted. Nietzsche at once comes to mind, and the impassioned critique of "ascetic ideals" in his *Genealogy of Morals*.[23] Faulkner, a Nietzschean? Certainly not, and yet when writing *Light in August* he was perhaps not far from sharing Nietzsche's assumption that in essence all religions were "systems of cruelty."

Puritanism, sexism, racism. What joins them is obviously more than ideological kinship: a structural homology, an identical functioning.[24]

Each of them generates an order by way of distinctions and disjunctions. Thus Puritanism, in accordance with the converging traditions of Christianity and Platonic idealism, reasserts the old dualistic patterns of Western thinking – reality and ideality, matter and spirit, body and soul – and radicalizes them in terms of the Calvinistic division of humanity into the elect and the reprobate. Sexism likewise takes advantage of sexual difference to disjoin masculine from feminine, and racism of a difference in skin color to separate white from black. The disjoining is, of course, anything but neutral. It is a matter of sorting out, of identifying, categorizing, and classifying. Its purpose is the production of a workable taxonomy, which in turn will lead to a mandatory hierarchy of values.

One divides to oppose: ideal versus real, male versus female, white versus black. One term in the binary opposition is always valued over the other. Whereas ideality, masculinity, and whiteness are exalted, their opposites are abased. To divide is to pass judgment, to name the categories of good and evil, to assign them to fixed locations, and to draw between them boundaries not to be crossed. On the good side, *inside*, the clear, clean, orderly space of all that is valuable; on the other, *outside*, the alien, enemy territories of darkness and disorder, the abject kingdom of evil.

To enforce these divisions in society and ensure their maintenance, it is important that they should be guaranteed by solid barriers blocking off all circulation, all communication between what has been ordered to be kept apart. A society founded on rigid divisions and arbitrary exclusions can only be a *closed* society,[25] regulated by immutable taboos and demanding from its members total subjection to its law. Personal identity is never in any circumstances a mere matter of individual preference, but in a closed society there is no choice at all. Identities are defined and distributed according to the prevalent codes: everyone must be tied to a class, a race, a gender. To have a clear-cut identity is a social imperative. *Either/or:* male or female, white or black, elect or non-elect. Above or below.

Small wonder, then, that any sign of ambiguity, any swerve from the straight path of conformity, should be interpreted as a potential threat to the established order. Nothing is more detestable and more alarming to such a society than the in-between, the intermingled, the impure – that which blurs its neat fictions and undermines its dogmatic certainties. Characteristically, in the community of Jefferson, all illicit contacts are perceived as *contagions,* all breaches of rule as *defilements,* all punishments as *purgations,* and the threat posed to it by such figures as Hightower, Joanna, and Christmas is indeed that of their ambiguity. Joanna, the "nigger lover," is not quite a woman, at any rate not a white Southern woman (though she becomes a martyr of Southern womanhood in the public legend created after her death); Hightower, the unfrocked minister suspected both of being a homosexual and of having slept with a black woman, is not quite a man. It is Christmas, however, who provokes the greatest outrage:

> "He never acted like either a nigger or a white man. That was it. That was what made the folks so mad. For him to be a murderer and all dressed up and walking the town like he dared them to touch him, when he ought to have have been skulking and hiding in the woods, muddy and dirty and running. It was like he never even knew he was a murderer, let alone a nigger too." (p. 331)

These are the comments of the "town" on Christmas's behavior at Mottstown shortly before his capture. They express amazement, indignation, and a deep sense of malaise. The mere existence of Christmas has suddenly become an unbearable scandal, but what renders it so scandalous is not that he is assumed to be the black rapist and murderer of a white woman; it is rather the fact that everything in him denies that assumption. What makes "the folks so mad" is not the presumed miscegenation, the guilty mixture of black and white blood, but the lack in Christmas of any trace of miscegenation, the visible invisibility of his blackness. This "nigger" is white; the blackness in his whiteness cannot be ascertained. Neither his physical aspect nor his style of behavior conforms to racist stereotypes. Now if a black man can look and act exactly like a white man, if appearances fail to match and confirm essences, whiteness and blackness alike become shady notions, and once the white/black opposition has broken down, the whole social structure threatens to crumble. Christmas is thus a living challenge to the community's elemental norms and categories. Whether on purpose or not, whether knowingly or not, he subverts its either/or logic, draws attention to the fragility of the law, and points to the unacknowledged origin of racism by showing it up as a *cosa mentale,* a mere thing of the mind.

Christmas must therefore die without further delay. Yet the account of his ignominious death at the hands of Percy Grimm, the tribal god's avenging "angel" (437), suggests some kind of ritual murder rather than simple retaliation. Moreover, the highly rhetorical description of Christmas's last agony announces the posthumous transfiguration of the sacrificial victim by collective memory (see 439–40). As in all scapegoat ceremonies, a reversal seems to have taken place: from *agos,* a figure of defilement, Christmas has turned into *pharmakos,* a collector of communal guilt and agent of purification, and at the point of death he is reborn into myth. For all of his associations with Christ and the Passion, however, Christmas can hardly be said to serve a cathartic or redemptive purpose. Violence does not put an end to violence, it breeds further violence and further guilt, and for the closed society to persevere in its closedness, for the distinction between a pure inside and a corrupt outside to be reaffirmed and maintained, there will have to be other expulsions and other "crucifixions."

In *Tristes Tropiques* Claude Lévi-Strauss distinguishes two opposing types of society: *anthropoemic* societies (from the Greek *emein,* to vomit) and *anthropophagic* ones (from the Greek *phagein,* to digest).[26] Whereas the former expel their deviants by "vomiting" them into prisons and asylums or by putting them to death, the latter absorb and "digest" them by assigning a specific function to them within the community. The society portrayed by Faulkner in

Light in August obviously belongs to the first category, and given the importance of nausea in his fiction, the vomiting metaphor seems here particularly relevant. Like Faulkner's many self-tormented idealists, from Horace Benbow in *Sanctuary* to David Levine in *A Fable*, this society becomes sick whenever it is confronted with its "others" and ends up vomiting what it cannot digest: *intolerance* in every possible sense, including the medical one.

Light in August may be read in many ways, and it would be mistaken, assuredly, to reduce it to a piece of fictionalized sociology. Yet it would be just as wrong to read Faulkner's novels as timeless evocations of a supposedly unchanging human condition. Faulkner wrote about specific people in specific places, and he did so in full awareness of his complex Southern experience. He took no shortcut to universality. And if his fiction illuminates "the human heart in conflict with itself," it also tells us a good deal about the inner conflicts of the culture in which he lived. Revealingly, his very best novels, from *The Sound and the Fury* through *Absalom, Absalom!* and *The Hamlet* to *Go Down, Moses*, are all Yoknapatawpha novels, and they all probe and scan the South, past and present, with ruthless sharpness and thoroughness. *Light in August* has its place among them. It is probably not Faulkner's greatest book, but as a radiograph of the South in the late twenties and early thirties it stands as a unique achievement.

NOTES

1. The absence of family ties was noted as early as 1949 by Phyllis Hirshleifer in "As Whirlwinds in the South: An Analysis of *Light in August*," *Perspective* 2 (Summer 1949):225–38. On this point see also Alfred Kazin, "The Stillness of *Light in August*," *Partisan Review* 24 (Autumn 1957):519–38.
2. See Brooks, *William Faulkner: The Yoknapatawpha Country* (New Haven, Conn.: Yale University Press, 1963), p. 47.
3. Brooks, *William Faulkner*, p. 69.
4. On the concept of anomie in social theory and its ideological implications, see Alvin W. Gouldner, *The Coming Crisis of Western Sociology* (New York: Avon Books, 1970).

5. See Brooks's observations on this point (of honor?) in *William Faulkner*, pp. 51–2.

6. See *LIA*, 272: "So the hatless men, who had deserted counters and desks, swung down, even including the one who ground the siren. They came too and were shown several different places where the sheet had lain, and some of them with pistols already in their pockets began to canvass about for someone to crucify."

7. It is remarkable that the manuscript version of chapter 5 includes references to Christmas's "black blood" and "Negro smell," which Faulkner removed only when he wrote the final text. On this point, see Regina K. Fadiman, *Faulkner's "Light in August": A Description and Interpretation of the Revisions* (Charlottesville: University Press of Virginia, 1975), pp. 42–3.

8. *Faulkner in the University: Class Conferences at the University of Virginia, 1957–1958*, ed. Frederick L. Gwynn and Joseph L. Blotner (Charlottesville: University of Virginia Press, 1959), p. 72.

9. When asked by Joanna how he knows that one of his parents was "part nigger," Joe admits that he does not know and adds with sardonic bitterness: "If I'm not [a nigger], damned if I haven't wasted a lot of time" (*LIA*, 240–1).

10. This, according to the narrator, is what he then "might have thought" had he been older: "*That is why I am different from the others: because he is watching me all the time*" (*LIA*, 129). The scenes at the orphanage remind one of the transformation of an innocent child into an abject monster that Sartre describes in his *Saint Genet* (Paris: Gallimard, 1952). Sartre remarks in this connection that "the gaze of adults is a *constitutive power* which has changed [Genet] into a *constituted nature*" (*Saint Genet*, p. 55). Between Genet's childhood and Christmas's there are several intriguing analogies: the former, at seven, was committed to the charge of Morvan peasants; the latter, at five, is adopted by a couple of Mississippi farmers.

11. Alfred Kazin defines Christmas as "an abstraction seeking to become a human being" ("The Stillness of *Light in August*," p. 524). It is rather the other way round: Christmas is a human being seeking not to become an abstraction. Faulkner criticism treats him all too often as if he were a human cipher or an arch-villain, or regards him as a character totally bent on self-destruction. Thadious M. Davis is closer to the truth when she notes that "Joe's refusal, though effectively defeated, is a positive, progressive impulse, but one doomed to failure because it cuts so sharply against the grain of traditional southern life

and thought." See *Faulkner's "Negro": Art and the Southern Context* (Baton Rouge: Louisiana State University Press, 1983), p. 133.

12. See *LIA*, 275: "It was as if all their individual five senses had become one organ of looking, like an apotheosis."

13. For a perceptive discussion of Joanna, see R. G. Collins, "*Light in August:* Faulkner's Stained-Glass Triptych," *Mosaic* 7 (Fall 1973):122–30.

14. On the role of paternity in Faulkner's fiction, see my essay, "Fathers in Faulkner," in *The Fictional Father: Lacanian Readings of the Text*, ed. Robert Con Davis (Amherst: University of Massachusetts Press, 1981), pp. 115–46.

15. For a more detailed discussion of the toothpaste episode, see my *Parcours de Faulkner* (Paris: Ophrys, 1982), pp. 300–1.

16. According to *"Light in August": A Concordance to the Novel*, ed. Jack L. Capps (Faulkner Concordance Advisory Board, 1979), "dark" occurs 134 times, "darkness" 35 times. It is also worth recalling that Faulkner's working title for the novel was "Dark House."

17. Similarly, as Byron Bunch runs to the cabin where Lena lies in labor, he hears her wail and cry "in a tongue unknown to man" (*LIA*, 378). Motherhood, it seems, has its own, inaccessible code.

18. It is noteworthy that, just like Addie in *As I Lay Dying*, Joanna feels the need to *stage* her sin, as if speech and theatrics were required to make it real. During her fits of nymphomania she shows "an avidity for the forbidden wordsymbols" (*LIA*, 244) and adopts "such formally erotic attitudes and gestures as a Beardsley of the time of Petronius might have drawn" (*LIA*, 245). Filth is only filth once named; sin is a role to be played. Hence the necessity of turning fornication into a series of "faultlessly played scenes" (*LIA*, 249). "The obscene," as Gilles Deleuze has pointed out, "is not the intrusion of the body into language but their common reflection." See *Logique du sens* (Paris: Editions de Minuit, 1969), p. 326.

19. Many critical studies have been devoted to this aspect of the novel. The most useful is still Ilse Dusoir Lind's "The Calvinistic Burden of *Light in August*," *New England Quarterly* 30 (September 1957):307–29.

20. See Weber, *The Protestant Ethic and the Spirit of Capitalism*, trans. Talcott Parsons (New York: Scribners, 1930); this influential essay first appeared in 1904–5.

21. See Weber, *Protestant Ethic*, p. 95.

22. In this passage the narrative is handled in such a way as to make it

impossible to distinguish the narrator's from Hightower's point of view. The perspective here is dual or mixed.

23. Consider, for instance, the following reflections:" [A]n ascetic life is a self-contradiction: here rules *ressentiment* without equal, that of an insatiable instinct and power-will that wants to become master not over something in life but over life itself, over its most profound, powerful, and basic conditions; here an attempt is made to employ force to block up the wells of force; here physiological well-being itself is viewed askance, and especially the outward expression of this well-being, beauty and joy; while pleasure is felt and *sought* in ill-constitutedness, decay, pain, mischance, ugliness, voluntary deprivation, self-mortification, self-flagellation, self-sacrifice." *On the Genealogy of Morals,* trans. Walter Kaufmann (New York: Vintage Books, 1969), pp. 117–18. There is scarcely a sentence in this passage that could not be applied to Faulkner's novel.

24. See John Tucker, "William Faulkner's *Light in August:* Toward a Structuralist Reading," *Modern Language Quarterly* 43 (June 1982): 138–55.

25. The distinction between an "open society" and a "closed society" was first made by Henri Bergson in *Les Deux Sources de la morale et de la religion* (1932). These terms were reused in a different, secular and rationalistic, sense by Karl R. Popper: "the closed society is characterized by the belief in magical taboos, while the open society is one in which men have learned to be to some extent critical of taboos, and to base decisions on the authority of their own intelligence" (*The Open Society and Its Enemies,* 5th ed. [Princeton, N.J.: Princeton University Press, 1966], Vol. I, p. 202). My own use of the phrase refers back to Popper. It is interesting to note that Popper's definition of the closed society, in its emphasis on the latter's "semi-organic" character (see p. 173), amounts to a liberal's unsympathetic redefinition of Brooks's "community." It may also be worth recalling that *Mississippi: The Closed Society* is the title that the historian James W. Silver gave to his study of racial disturbances in Faulkner's home state during the early sixties. The book was published in 1964 by Harcourt, Brace & World.

26. See *Tristes Tropiques,* trans. John Russell (New York: Atheneum, 1968), p. 386.

5

The Women of *Light in August*

JUDITH BRYANT WITTENBERG

A SKED whether he found it easier to create male or female characters, Faulkner told a student at the University of Virginia, "It's much more fun to try to write about women because I think women are marvelous, they're wonderful, and I know very little about them, and so I just – it's much more fun to try to write about women than about men – more difficult, yes."[1] The mingling of veneration and mystification in Faulkner's response seems to reflect an attitude in which enthusiastic interest is grounded in bemusement. On other occasions, however, he revealed that some of his novels, now among those regarded as his finest, had their inception in visions of individual women: *The Sound and the Fury*, for example, was inspired by the mental picture of a little girl climbing a pear tree in her muddy drawers to look in at the window of the room where her grandmother lies dead, and *Light in August* "began with Lena Grove, the idea of the young girl with nothing, pregnant, determined to find her sweetheart. It was – that was out of my admiration for women, for the courage and endurance of women. As I told that story I had to get more and more into it, but that was mainly the story of Lena Grove."[2] That women in general captured Faulkner's imagination and that specific women, real or imaginary, inspired some of his strongest writing can hardly be doubted, but what does remain in question is how to assess the fictional portraits of women that result.

Light in August offers a striking case in point, for at one level it exhibits Faulkner's ability to understand and portray women struggling with the limitations imposed upon them by a restrictive Southern society and by the very nature of the human condition, whereas at another it embodies the potential for reviving the old argument about whether Faulkner is a misogynist or an admirer of women — both because many of the female characters simultaneously fascinate and terrify the men with whom they come in contact and because their portrayals can sometimes be interpreted as circumscribed and reductive. Nevertheless, it is part of the richness of *Light in August* that it so variously depicts members of both sexes desperately attempting to come to terms with the ideas about gender that have been imposed upon them by the culture in which they have come to maturity. The women of the novel — like the men — are at once psychologically distinctive individuals and emblems of the ongoing difficulties human beings have with socially conditioned concepts of masculinity and femininity and with questions of appropriate behavior in which gender is an issue. Moreover, the novel as a whole reveals in intriguing ways the problematic presence of the "feminine" as an informing principle, the term "feminine" denoting that which is dependent, emotional, and marginal — just as "masculine" is that which is independent, rational, and culture-centered.

In some respects, Faulkner's recognition of the general plight of women in the fictional world of *Light in August* — at once timeless and time-bound — makes it tempting to read the novel as proto-feminist. Byron Bunch, for example, comments on Hightower's obsession with his dead grandfather as an instance of the sort of unfortunate thing "that men do to the women who belong to them . . . that is why women have to be strong and should not be held blameable for what they do with or for or because of men, since God knew that being anybody's wife was a tricky enough business" (56), and the novel portrays throughout the difficulties encountered by all women who are in some sense belongings of the men they marry — or simply of a patriarchal society with rigid conceptions of women's essential nature and of what constitutes appropriate behavior in a female. Some of the men, such as Gail Hightower and Nathaniel Burden, see their wives solely as instruments of their own designs, paying no heed to the women's individual needs unless forced to do so; others, like Armstid, view their spouses from a wary distance with a mixture of fear and reluctant admiration. Virtually all of the men have strong ideas about "their" women and about women in general, and Faulkner sometimes depicts the operations of such thinking in ways that reveal a certain sympathy with its targets. So the contemporary Southern concept of virginity as necessary in an unmarried woman – a concept originating, as the psychoanalyst Karen Horney has pointed out, in the male wish to "ensure some measure of 'sexual thraldom' " in a wife-to-be[3] – crumbles with ludicrous ease at the moment when Byron falls in love with the pregnant but single Lena Grove, "contrary to all the tradition of his austere and jealous country raising which demands in the object physical inviolability" (44).

Although the veneration of virginity was openly restrictive, creating problems for any woman who willingly or inadvertently transgressed it, more subtle difficulties were engendered by such conventions as the praise of maternity. After seeing Lena with her newborn child, Hightower thinks of her admiringly, musing on the "young strong body from out whose travail even there shone something tranquil and unafraid" and on what he now sees as *"her life, her destiny. The good stock peopling in tranquil obedience to it the good earth; from these hearty loins without hurry or haste descending mother and daughter"* (384). Hightower's warm regard has a nether side, however, for he is tacitly circumscribing Lena's potential by viewing her as biologically determined: childbearing may be personally gratifying for a woman, even as it fulfills the need of the human race to perpetuate itself, but it is only one aspect of the female experience – as Lena herself seems to recognize when she seeks to evade or at least delay her female fate by engaging in travel and seeing the world. Although males are the principal proponents of ideas that overtly or implicitly limit the ways women are seen and permitted to behave, women themselves readily, if unconsciously, internalize them – like the "good women" of Jefferson who have "plenty of time to smell out sin" and thus are quick to condemn the peccadilloes of Hightower's wife (61). Faulkner's "good women" are characteristically those who have accepted patriarchal prescriptions, and their treatment of members of their own sex, as depicted in works like *Light in August* and *Sanctuary*, may be no less pernicious than the treatment women receive from men.

These assumptions about the nature and importance of vir-

ginity, maternity, and virtue are inseparable from the social conditioning to which both men and women are subjected and that
ultimately affects, almost always in restrictive fashion, their vision
of the people around them. As the narrator says, elucidating the
process by which we project our own tendencies upon others in a
narrowminded manner: "Man knows so little about his fellows. In
his eyes all men or women act upon what he believes would
motivate him if he were mad enough to do what that other man or
woman is doing" (43). This conceptual projection is obviously
cruel and dehumanizing in a number of ways, becoming evident at
the most basic level in the tendency of people to label each other.
Such labeling has particular implications for women in that – as
Dale Spender has pointed out in her work on the linguistic foundations of patriarchy – there exist in English many negative words
for females without semantic equivalents for males, and such verbal derogation of women both constructs female inferiority and
helps to confirm it.[4] In *Light in August*, as in other of Faulkner's
works, the readiness of people to label women as "whore" or
"nonvirgin" or "menopausal" or "sexually repressed" limits their
ability to truly see them as individuals, and this has implications
for nearly every woman depicted. When Joe Christmas calls Bobbie Allen his whore or derides Joanna Burden's menopausal state,
or when the town becomes focused on Joanna's spinsterhood or
Mrs. Hightower's alleged sexual frustration, they are all failing to
see the women "in the round," as the complex beings they actually are. Certainly some of Faulkner's men are also harshly labeled, but there seems to be a greater number of reductive categories for the women.

   In portraying the roles of such ideas and labels in circumscribing
women's lives, Faulkner could be said to be aligning himself with
those sympathetic to their plight, but other aspects of *Light in
August* suggest that he might have been caught up in stereotypical
ways of thinking. For one thing, in this novel supposedly inspired
by his sense of a specific woman and by admiration for women in
general, we have but little access to female subjectivity and sensibility – as is also true of an earlier female-centered work, *The
Sound and the Fury,* in which Caddy Compson is presented only in
an oblique way, through the eyes of her brothers. In *Light in August*

Faulkner does offer some brief, unmediated depictions of women, but his central female figure, Lena Grove, is seen primarily through the consciousness of the males who respond to and discuss her; the other women characters share the same "fate" in that there is limited direct portrayal of any of them.

To be sure, Faulkner opens the novel with a delineation of Lena's early and recent history that gives us temporary access to her inner life and an awareness of her individuality. This is immediately followed, however, by Armstid's and Winterbottom's speculations about her situation and by a number of other scenes in which two men discuss her at some length, a technique that distances us from her and serves to suggest the way in which she is defined and "contained" by male speech and male perceptions. In one of these scenes, Byron confidently analyzes what he sees as her paradoxical response to Lucas Burch, in which her awareness of the fact that he is a "scoundrel" coexists with a determination to be with him "when the right time comes" (285). In another such scene, Byron and Hightower gently discuss the impending birth of Lena's child in a long dialogue that also contains a despairing comment about the ways in which "men have suffered from good women" (299), thus simultaneously revealing a gallant protectiveness toward a specific woman and a tendency to dismissive generalizations about the gender — attitudes apparently very different but both in fact rooted in categorical thinking.

Something similar happens with Mrs. Hines, whose reaction to the capture of Christmas is discussed by two men and who is theorized about with a high degree of confidence by Gavin Stevens. Faulkner is, of course, concerned to depict the pervasiveness of gossip and discussion as the local inhabitants respond to major events and assess their more intriguing visitors, and one of his characters muses about the way in which, "in a small town, where evil is harder to accomplish, where opportunities for privacy are scarcer, . . . people can invent more of it in other people's names" (65–6). Still, the fact is that male words and perceptions tend to dominate the novel and serve as the filter through which the women are viewed. Moreover, even Lena's first long direct monologue is little more than a recounting of a rationale for Lucas's disappearance that was obviously provided for her by Lucas himself — a male verbal construct accepted by a woman and propounded as her own — and the moment in which Byron and Lucas come to blows over her, though echoing a myriad of such moments in fiction and in life, suggests how powerfully Lena's fate is — or at least is assumed to be — in male hands. Male words and actions serve tacitly to control her at every level; that she eludes them at several points to assert her own quiddity and her right to act as she wishes is a major triumph.

Another aspect of *Light in August* that reveals Faulkner as perhaps subconsciously caught up in the sort of categorical thinking that the novel explicitly exposes and derides is the fact that his narrator tends to generalize about women but not about men. Passages mentioning the "natural female infallibility for the spontaneous comprehension of evil" (117) or asserting "that the woman observes no rules of physical combat" (222) serve strongly to suggest that the narrator is indeed a "he." At the same time, our responses to these elements are infinitely complicated and enriched by the novel's central portrait of a man who undergoes in his early years what might be called a "female" experience. Just as women are often initially judged by men solely as physical objects, so Joe Christmas is first viewed by his adoptive father as a thing, looked at with "the same stare with which he might have examined a horse or a second hand plow, convinced beforehand that he would see flaws, convinced beforehand that he would buy" (133). In subsequent scenes Joe is pressured to give up his surname, infused with the patriarchal Law in the form of the Presbyterian catechism, and dismissively labeled by Max as "Romeo" or "The Beale Street Playboy" (199). These experiences are analogous to those constantly undergone by women, and the fact that Joe refuses some, struggles continuously with others, and finally himself begins to categorize and demean women only serves to underscore the importance of such experiences as part of the process by which males and females are subjected to, and consequently either internalize or reject, certain deindividualizing and oppressive conceptions.

If Faulkner presents us with unsettling ambiguities in thus depicting (and possibly at some tacit level subscribing to) some of the patterns of thinking and acting that serve to define women in negative ways, in his individual portraits of women in *Light in August* he shows with brutal directness the problems they encounter within the overwhelmingly patriarchal society of Jefferson. Virtually all of the women in the novel are actively mistreated or subtly restricted by the mores of the community in which they live, and a number of them attempt to assert themselves or to rebel, sometimes in destructive ways. Faulkner makes clear that such problems are not limited to the one sex – that comparable difficulties are encountered by men who have not been fully assimilated into the patriarchy because of their uncertain sexuality, their racial antecedents, or their psychological handicaps – but the varied plights of the female characters serve collectively as an indictment of the restrictive context in which women must struggle to find themselves and to survive.

Among the minor female characters, most are married and many are so thoroughly identified with their husbands that we never learn their first names; the text echoes the people of the town in simply referring to them as "Mrs." This was, of course, a common practice of the time, but it has the general effect of denying these women a strong portion of their individuality, embodied at one level in the Christian name bestowed upon them by their parents. Although marriage is considered by the patriarchy to be the proper destiny for women – indeed, the only socially validated one – Faulkner shows that it is no panacea. In *Light in August* the lives of the married females are often hard. Mrs. Armstid, characterized by the "savage" gray twist of hair at the back of her head and the brusqueness of her dealings with men and women alike, has undergone the grueling experience of bearing five children in six years and of preparing three meals a day for thirty years, rarely leaving her isolated farmhouse. Her angry comments about "you durn men" (14) are hardly surprising, and her grudging kindness to Lena Grove reveals a tacit recognition of sisterhood with the young woman whose pregnancy and arduous trip in search of her man are reminders of her own trials of the past. Mrs. Beard, the boarding house proprietor, is one of the few women of the novel to know any sort of economic independence, even though her income may be minimal and her occupation closely allied with traditional female domestic roles. She aligns herself, however, with Mrs. Armstid in offering reluctant assistance to the young Lena and in denouncing "you men," who "cant even know your own limits for devilment" (396). Both women are caught between their knowledge that the role of a "good woman" requires rejection of Lena as a social pariah and their piercing awareness that her plight, like theirs, has been engendered by men, whether well intentioned or not. Their verbal outbursts against the opposite sex, if ultimately unproductive, are obviously deeply felt.

Two other married women of the novel, their lives similarly full of toil and confinement, engage in mini-rebellions that are more than simply rhetorical. Mrs. McEachern of the "beaten face" seems prematurely aged by her difficult marriage, and she has been virtually effaced as an individual, forced to view the world through a filter created by the powerful ideas and personality of her husband. Her appearance, with "something queer about her eyes," suggests to an observer that "whatever she saw or heard, she saw or heard through a more immediate manshape or manvoice, as if she were the medium and the vigorous and ruthless husband the control" (138). Her husband and Joe ignore her during their intense confrontations – "[n]either of them so much as looked at her" during one such scene (139) – as if taking it for granted that the only transactions of real importance are those that occur between men. Although Mrs. McEachern has been "hammered" by such experiences "into an attenuation of dumb hopes and frustrated desires" (155), she finds ways to make her presence felt, providing succor to Joe when he has been brutalized by her husband, lying on his behalf, and offering up her pitiful savings. Joe, like her husband, violently rejects her efforts, shoving her literally and figuratively aside, but her efforts are significant in showing that her impulses to assert her values, to nurture and protect, have not been totally extinguished by a life spent in the presence of overwhelming and heedless men who prize toughness and austerity, devaluing all things soft and implicitly "feminine" in the process.

Mrs. Hines is a similar example of a downtrodden wife who makes brief but admirable attempts to come into her own, and for a time she is more successful than Mrs. McEachern. For more than thirty years she has been completely subdued by her fanatical husband, almost invisible as well as utterly passive. "Hardly ever

110

seen" for decades by the townspeople (324), she has, astonishingly, refrained from questioning Hines about their dead daughter's missing child. An intuition that Joe Christmas may be that child, however, elicits long-hidden strengths and a surprising degree of determination. The moment in which she physically supports her husband after one violent outburst foreshadows the scene in which she psychologically takes charge, emerging from her house in the flamboyant purple dress and plumed hat that signal her new assertiveness and leading her husband on a dogged quest for her newly discovered grandson. She even – in this novel dominated by male language – begins to speak at some length, although she occasionally sounds "as if she were a puppet and the voice that of a ventriloquist in the next room" (359), so long has she been dominated by her controlling husband. Her voice seems disused, she appears surprised at the sound of it, and the men soon reclaim the rhetorical stage. Late in the novel, as she sits with Lena's baby on her lap, Mrs. Hines has returned to a state of impotent silence, appearing "dumb, beastlike, as though she did not understand English" (381); in a moment of consummate pathos she seems to lose even her grip on reality, assuming erroneously that the baby is her great-grandchild. Her earlier self-assertion has been nonetheless significant: Some of her wishes have been heeded, and her narration of the events of the past has imbued them with some sort of meaning and order. She has, perhaps, in an experience more common to Faulkner's male characters, learned that the process of storytelling can bring the teller valuable rewards. As Gavin Stevens suggests, in the moments of telling her tale after years of silence "very likely she learned it herself then for the first time, actually saw it whole and real at the same time" (422). Her life may be as unsatisfying as before, but she has possibly gained the kinds of insights that would align her with other Faulknerian tellers such as Quentin Compson of *Absalom, Absalom!*, who finds himself at the end of his narration still overwhelmed by anguished ambivalence toward his native region but fully aware of the satisfactions of playing an active role in the imaginative re-creation of its history.

The married woman whose plight and rebellious response to it are the most dramatic is, of course, Mrs. Hightower. In what was probably an early version of the novel, Faulkner made her an actual character; his altering of her presentation from direct portrayal to an indistinct memory in her husband's psyche and in the minds of the bemused townspeople does little to mitigate the symbolic force of her narrative. The recounting of her tragic experience early in the novel not only illuminates the guilty isolation in which Hightower now lives, it provides us with a paradigm of the potential destruction that a woman of energy and frustrated desires may undergo. Coming to the town as a hopeful young minister's wife, Mrs. Hightower soon learns that she has little claim on her husband's attention because of his immersion in a strange admixture of religion and ancestor worship, obsessions that he cannot get "untangled from each other, even in the pulpit" (56). She becomes increasingly alienated from him and from the townspeople, until anger finally causes her violent and blasphemous outburst during a church service. Mrs. Hightower is quickly dispatched to a sanatorium, any disruptive behavior by a woman being promptly designated as derangement in those days, as Phyllis Chesler has pointed out in her work on women and madness,[5] even though such behavior might simply constitute an understandably aggressive rejection of the "feminine" roles being forced upon her by her husband and the larger society. Her "cure" involves capitulation to the standards of conduct expected of her by the community of Jefferson. After some months of institutionalization, during which neither her husband nor his congregation show more than the most desultory interest in her progress, she returns temporarily subdued, "chastened" and attempting to act "like the ladies had wanted her to be all the time, as they believed that the minister's wife should be. She attended church and prayer meeting regularly, and the ladies called upon her and she called upon them, sitting quiet and humble" (60).

Mrs. Hightower's "cure" doesn't take, however, and her final actions involve openly adulterous sex in a Memphis hotel and suicide of a sort calculated to cause her husband the greatest possible public embarrassment. She makes sure that her identity is known by leaving her name on a piece of paper in the hotel room, only to have the newspapers underscore the nature of her fundamental problems by referring to her simply as "wife of the Reverend Gail Hightower" (62). Mrs. Hightower's dissatisfactions and ultimate fate are reminiscent of Edna Pontellier's rebellious "awakening" in Kate Chopin's 1899 novel, specifically of the way in which she scandalizes New Orleans society by her extramarital liaisons and self-inflicted death by drowning. The lives of both women, though in one way clearly and pointlessly self-destructive, constitute a resounding refusal to conform to restrictive community mores or to tolerate their husbands' self-absorbed failure to comprehend their complex needs and psychological makeup. That Faulkner's Reverend Hightower ultimately comes to understand his own culpability in the matter – the fact that "he did not see her at all because of the face which he had already created in his mind" (454) and had used her merely as "an instrument to be called to Jefferson" (463) – only increases the poignancy of his wife's case. Her early decision to use marriage as a means to escape the confining circumstances in which she found herself as a result of her birth and upbringing ironically only serves to trap her in an extremely frustrating relationship, driving her to a rebellion that ends in tragedy.

Faulkner thus vividly and variously portrays the ways in which the married women who have supposedly fulfilled the role decreed for them by society are nevertheless frustratingly trapped. Two of the unmarried women, though gainfully employed and sexually active, and hence seemingly free of the constrictions suffered by their older married counterparts, are also subject to confusion and self-imposed defeat, primarily because their instincts are at war with their socially received ideas. The waitress-prostitute, Bobbie Allen, with whom Joe Christmas experiences his first intimacies, seems at the outset hard, suffering from an "inner corruption" (161), but she quickly and with rough kindness responds to Joe's compelling needs, ignoring his ineptness and inexperience. She subsequently "falls" from the relative innocence of their connection – turning her back on the way it has temporarily restored in her the ability to react to a man as a suitor rather than as the purchaser of her services – when she shows herself to be an instrument of the social code that devalues anyone with black blood, turning her anger from the true culprit to Joe himself, calling him "a nigger son of a bitch," and standing by as her friends beat him up (204–5). Joe has been previously and similarly betrayed by another young woman, the dietitian Miss Atkins, whose urgent sexuality is at odds with her fear of being caught and censured and who projects her distress and confusion on the young boy, an innocent bystander. Sexually responsive both to the amorous young intern who attempts to seduce her and later to the auto-erotic feel of the sheets on her naked body, the dietitian is also terrified of being discovered during an intimate encounter, for she knows that her sexual activity will be condemned by the middle-class mores of which she is essentially a prisoner. Realizing that Joe has been present at her sexual liaison and guiltily aware of Doc Hines's denunciation of "bitchery" and "womanfilth" (123–4), she desperately tries the varying strategies of bribery, anger, and finally banishment in order to rid herself of the reminder of her "sin" against social and professional values. As in the previous instance, Joe is the immediate victim, but the larger culprit is a rigid system of standards for judging individuals.

Ironically, an unmarried woman who suffers mightily at the hands of the patriarchy is also barely acknowledged by most of those to whom her tragedy is of the greatest significance. Milly Hines, important in narrative terms by virtue of her role as Joe Christmas's mother and the daughter of the Hineses, and in symbolic terms as a victim of restrictive ideas about race and women's sexuality, receives only passing mention in the text and is never invoked by her son. Her story is, however, paradigmatic at every level, albeit in such an extreme way that it becomes almost a parody of the womanly plight. Enticed from her repressive home at the age of eighteen by the promptings of her own sexual desire and the itinerant exoticism of a circus employee, Milly directly confronts – and dies at the hands of – a system embodied in her obsessive and heartless father. Doc Hines dismisses Milly's asser-tion that her lover is Mexican, saying he "knowed better," even as he harshly labels his own daughter as "God's abomination of womanflesh" and his own wife as a "whore's dam," hitting both when they attempt to defy him or to deflect his pursuit and murder of the circus man (353, 358). Hines's final crime against his daughter is willfully to allow her to die in childbirth and then to dispose of her child; subsequently her own son effaces even the idea of her from his memory. During Milly's brief life and tragic death, she serves comprehensively as an example of the sort of mistreatment women can receive at the hands of overpowering men, for she is confined, labeled, brutalized, and ultimately obliterated, both literally and figuratively.

In his presentation of these eight minor female characters, Faulkner dramatizes the imposition of social proscriptions on particular women and the ways in which those women respond psychologically along a spectrum that ranges from utter passivity or victimization to constructive rebellion and thence to self-destructive excess. But Faulkner's portrayals of Lena Grove and Joanna Burden – the central figures whose stories are intimately linked with and serve to illuminate, directly or by contrast, those of the male characters – require a more complex assessment. Their stories are, like those of the other women, exemplary in crucial ways, but they are also more difficult to interpret simply as socially realistic, proto-feminist portrayals of women profoundly affected by a restrictive social system.

Lena Grove, for example, is certainly capable of being analyzed in social-psychological terms as the product of an orphaned and exploited childhood in which she was forced to care for her older brother's children and to do his housework, as eventually finding solace with a man who impregnated and abandoned her, and as managing to survive through such defense mechanisms as passive-aggressiveness, denial, patience, and mordant humor. But she no less certainly warrants discussion as a mythic figure, as a virtual earth goddess. Faulkner himself spoke of her "pagan quality," comparing her to the women "on whom Jupiter begot children,"[6] and critics over the years have referred to her as symbolizing the "world of nature with its total indifference to both moral and social categories" or as constituting "a kind of impersonalised catalytic force, effecting change but itself unchanging."[7]

The familiar celebration of Lena Grove as some sort of mythic figure is not without its problems for the feminist reader, for, as Karen Horney has pointed out, such glorification of the female has its roots in the "dread of woman,"[8] an idea upon which Dorothy Dinnerstein elaborates in her discussion of the goddess as evincing man's feelings of awe, fear, and sometimes disgust toward things that are mysterious to him, such as a woman's fertile body.[9] This ambiguous celebration of the fecund female, of which Lena Grove is an early Faulknerian instance, finds its ultimate embodiment in the excessive portrait of Eula Varner in *The Hamlet,* with its almost nauseating overtones of womanly ripeness.

In *Light in August,* we see an intriguing struggle on the part of the narrator and characters such as Byron and Hightower between an effort to "read" Lena in realistic terms and a wish to regard her as an almost abstract force. In the early pages Lena is on the road, apprehensive that her child will be born before she finds Lucas, wishing to be thought "a lady," and tacitly refusing to hear facts that will undermine the consoling picture of her situation that she has created for herself – in short, a comprehensible young woman caught up in a conflict between private illusions and distressing external realities. At other points, however, she is depicted with a mythic overlay, as when the narrator describes her as advancing "like something moving forever and without progress across an urn" (5) or as traveling "with the untroubled unhaste of a change of season" (47). Even Byron's description of her as "a young woman betrayed and deserted" (48), though close to the facts, has the effect of moving our sense of her toward the abstract. By the end of the novel, even as we admire her ability to cope quietly with the birth of her baby in relative isolation and her refusal to make a hasty marriage for the sake of her "good name," we realize that she is leaving the community in the same impersonal, enigmatic way in which she arrived, as if she were some sort of detached visiting goddess. Lena seems at one and the same time an uncomprehending peasant with strong survival instincts and an elusive, almost mythic presence. This is not to say that Faulkner's double-layered presentation of Lena is anything but richly ambiguous, but rather to point out the ways in which it complicates our responses to, and assessments of, this pivotal female figure.

Joanna Burden, the other central woman character, also defies simple interpretation. Like Lena, she is an outsider in the community who faces problems created by an inconveniently aroused sexuality; also like Lena, her refusal to capitulate to the community's standards presents a radical challenge to those standards that makes onlookers uncomfortable. They deal with their discomfort

116

by labeling, denouncing, or ignoring her, and her murder is only a final violent reenactment of the sort of repudiation she has suffered throughout her lifetime. Unmarried, childless, and, worse, a patron of black causes, Joanna is at every level a threat to the values of the local white patriarchy; the site of her house, far outside the town, symbolizes her marginal social position. A recent study of attitudes in the Old South points out that there was, on the part of males, a pervasive "distrust of feminine brains" that manifested itself in a preference for the simple-hearted and uneducated young woman; at the same time, men and women alike regarded spinsterhood as a "form of social death."[10] In being intelligent, opinionated, and single, Joanna violates every aspect of the local social code for women. She is thus a "traitor" to her gender, a situation severely exacerbated by her treachery to her race because of her overt interest in ameliorating the plight of oppressed blacks. Both her innate qualities and the choices she has made inevitably condemn Joanna to pariahhood.

Psychologically, too, Joanna is a very complicated woman. Obviously she early became identified with her father, who taught her to see blacks as a "curse" for the sins of the white race and led her to devote much of her time and energy to being an advisor and benefactor to black schools and colleges; because her father had little interest in her mother, caring before their marriage only that she be "a good housekeeper" and "at least thirtyfive years old" (237), Joanna has also learned to repudiate the mothering potential in herself. When Joe first meets her, she responds with the "mantrained" habits of a lifetime, but their sexual liaison arouses the dormant "mother" within her and she becomes fully sensual, a woman in the throes of total, if temporary, dedication to the carnal life and manifesting a powerful, though belated, wish for a child. Joe sees her as a "dual personality" (221), at once pleasure-seeking female and ratiocinative controlling male, and though the inadequacies of such a categorization are evident from the start, Joanna does evince an ongoing internal struggle between the "father" and the "mother" that ends with a fatal reversion to some of the ideas of her own father, asking Joe to study with a black lawyer and praying to God the Father in penance for the sexual activity she now sees as sinful. The forceful psychological presence of her father has clearly been oppressive – the mother in her appearing so briefly – and Joanna's manipulation of Joe could be interpreted as having its roots in a wish to control and punish an actual man in revenge for the ways in which she herself has been thus affected, its self-destructive aspect perhaps originating in some unacknowledged need to "kill off" the father in her. The final moment in which she is seen alive visually embodies this aspect of her psychological problems, for although she is, for unclear motives, attempting with steely determination to murder Joe with an old pistol that may have been part of her paternal inheritance, she nonetheless appears primarily as a "shadow," implying that her individual substance has been undermined by her failure to find a healthily integrated pattern of ideas and behavior (267).

Joanna's mutilated corpse, with her head facing one way and her body the other, seems somehow emblematic of the conflicts that distorted her life and resulted in her death; her male and female parts proved fatally separate. Her "head," or her rational-intellectual masculine self, was dominant for many years, perpetuating the ideas of her father and showing an admirable ability to work daily at causes, to endure solitude, to meet with men as intellectual equals, and even to understand the killer of her grandfather and half-brother as "hav[ing] to act as the land where he was born had trained him to act" (241); her awareness of the importance of social conditioning makes it possible to feel that she might have acute insights into the role of such influences in her own complex case. But although Joanna's competence and wisdom are impressive, she has for decades ignored the nonrational aspects of living. Hence the sudden and unexpected eruptions of the demands of her female sexual self; her "body," so long suppressed, proves difficult to deal with, driving her to excesses that anger and alienate her lover. Faulkner's depiction of Joanna's late-awakening sexuality may have been inspired, as Ilse Lind has suggested, by his reading about premenopausal sexual hyperesthesia in a book by a Dr. Louis Berman.[11] In any case, responses by those around Joanna to her combination of gray hair and hypersexuality reveal how little the society is prepared to comprehend or accept it. Lucas chides Joe about his mistress's gray hair, and Joe himself first muses angrily about his discovery of her

menopausal condition, then brutally tells her, "You just got old
and it happened to you and now you are not any good anymore,"
striking her at the same moment (262). Male uneasiness with the
idea of an older woman who is not only sexually active but openly
libidinous betrays an attitude that is still common. In the image of
the "sexual grandmother," all the complicated and negative ideas
men have about women – and that in many cases women have
about themselves – come to the fore, and she is a type rarely
depicted in fiction or film. Joe and Lucas joke about or revile
Joanna, and even the text itself shows her desire as extreme to the
point of being repellent, describing her as "completely corrupted,"
writhing "in the wild throes of nymphomania," with "her
clothing half torn to ribbons upon her" and her "wild hair
. . . alive like octopus tentacles" (245). With such distaste for her
middle-aged sensuality so universally envinced, it is no wonder
that Joanna herself has such problems coming to terms with it.

Not only do Joanna's troubling eruption of female sexuality and
her dissevered body signify her individual plight, they also serve as
indices to the larger tensions in the novel. *Light in August* contains,
for a Faulkner novel – and perhaps for any novel written by a man
in the early twentieth century – an unusual number of references
to physiological processes such as menstruation, childbirth, and
menopause, and these facts of feminine physicality are related to
the more complicated presence of the Female. Cleanth Brooks
long ago pointed out that characters like Joe and Hightower are
notable for their "antifeminine attitude," their tendency to
"shrink from" women, and that all the Calvinists in the novel
show a "hatred of the female principle"[12]; François Pitavy has
more recently discussed the novel's recurrent symbolic association
of femininity and evil.[13] What this suggests is that Faulkner was
attempting to demonstrate, by depicting the particular struggles of
individual men and women, the larger difficulties that the female
poses for society as a whole. At one level, *Light in August* is
"about" the problematic feminine and the difficulties created
when individuals and society attempt to confront, to cope with,
and to incorporate it.

Nancy Chodorow has written tellingly and at length about the
ways in which males are conditioned to reject the mother in them-

selves, the feminine potential for dependency and emotionality, in favor of autonomy, rationality, and the father. Masculinity, in her terms, is thus that which is nonfeminine, not-the-mother.[14] The conflict between male and female, between masculine and feminine, is evident throughout *Light in August* and comes only obliquely to any sort of useful resolution. It is present in the difficulties the central male characters find in dealing not only with the actual females in their lives, whom they tend alternately to desire and to repudiate, but also with the womanly potential in themselves. Joe, orphaned, possibly part black, and passively dependent on a social system whose workings are mysterious to him, leads (as we saw earlier) the sort of marginal existence that might be called female, and his subsequent and often violent rejection of emotional tenderness and of such nurturing acts as feeding and button sewing is part of his effort to assert his maleness. Hightower, too, of epicene appearance and uncertain sexual prowess, subconsciously attempts to affirm his manhood by identifying with his horse-mounted grandfather and his vainglorious Civil War prank to the exclusion of all else. Both Joe and Hightower are so fearful of being overtaken by dependency needs that they go to the other extreme. Their failure to comprehend or to accept the female almost inevitably dooms them to confusion and isolation. Although these men experience the women in their lives as either betrayers or implacable forces they cannot understand or contain, at some level they must share the responsibility for those betrayals. Even Byron Bunch, the most integrated of the male characters, teeters on the brink of being hampered by his fears, as when his instant and intuitive connection with Lena is implicitly, if only momentarily, threatened by the fact that her condition violates "the tradition" – those rigid male ideas about virginity. All of these men are forced, consciously or unconsciously, to accept the feminine by the end of the novel. Ironically, Joe in some sense "becomes" female through the hideous experience of being castrated, and Hightower, in acting as a midwife to Lena's baby, agreeing to be named as the partner in a putative homosexual encounter with Joe, and honestly confronting his responsibility for the failure of his marriage and the death of his wife, learns to incorporate both the actual and the symbolic woman. Byron, in close attendance on the unmarried mother he both loves and feels responsibility for, seems the most androgynous of the lot, even though the ridiculousness of his situation prevents it from being affirmative in the fullest sense.

The final chapter, containing the story of Byron and Lena as told by the furniture dealer to his wife, though unnerving in its presentation of new and unrelated characters so late in the narrative, perhaps offers a kind of symbolic resolution of some of these gender-related issues. The section is, to be sure, composed primarily of male words, but the fact that a woman is present, offering comments and questions and providing visible evidence of humor and honest sexuality, serves to bring together the previously incompatible gender strands in a reassuring way. It constitutes a subtly bisexual whole – much as, late in Virginia Woolf's seminal feminist essay, *A Room of One's Own,* the informing vision of a man and woman getting into a taxi together serves to endorse the author's pivotal concept of the androgynous mind, one that unifies and balances the masculine and feminine principles.

Clearly, the women of *Light in August,* though in their various avatars serving as representatives of the manifold stresses and restrictions placed on females by the society of the period, must finally be seen as inextricable threads within a novelistic fabric that reveals in many ways the complex, sometimes disruptive operations of the feminine principle. Faulkner manages simultaneously to present an array of fascinating women responding in differing ways to a culture that alternately exalts and oppresses them, to counterpoint male and female characters in a balanced manner, to show some of them struggling toward human understanding, and, finally, to offer a resolution that – comically, perhaps, but nonetheless seriously – integrates the masculine and feminine in positive and heartening terms.

NOTES

1. *Faulkner in the University: Class Conferences at the University of Virginia, 1957–1958,* ed. Frederick L. Gwynn and Joseph L. Blotner (Charlottesville: University of Virginia Press, 1959), p. 45.

2. Ibid., pp. 17, 74.
3. Karen Horney, *Feminine Psychology* (New York: Norton, 1967), p. 95.
4. Dale Spender, *Man Made Language* (London: Routledge & Kegan Paul, 1980), pp. 16, 23.
5. Phyllis Chesler, *Women and Madness* (New York: Avon, 1973), p. 31.
6. Gwynn and Blotner, eds., *Faulkner in the University,* p. 199.
7. Olga Vickery, *The Novels of William Faulkner,* rev. ed. (Baton Rouge: Louisiana State University Press, 1964), p. 80; Michael Millgate, *The Achievement of William Faulkner* (New York: Random House, 1966), pp. 125–6.
8. Horney, *Feminine Psychology,* p. 136.
9. Dorothy Dinnerstein, *The Mermaid and the Minotaur* (New York: Harper & Row, 1976), p. 125.
10. Bertram Wyatt-Brown, *Southern Honor: Ethics and Behavior in the Old South* (New York: Oxford University Press, 1982), pp. 202, 238.
11. Ilse Dusoir Lind, "Faulkner's Women," in *The Maker and the Myth: Faulkner and Yoknapatawpha, 1977,* ed. Evans Harrington and Ann J. Abadie (Jackson: University Press of Mississippi, 1978), pp. 95–6.
12. Cleanth Brooks, *William Faulkner: The Yoknapatawpha Country* (New Haven, Conn.: Yale University Press, 1963), pp. 56, 65.
13. François Pitavy, *Faulkner's "Light in August,"* trans. Gillian E. Cook (Bloomington: Indiana University Press, 1973), pp. 101, 140.
14. Nancy Chodorow, *The Reproduction of Mothering* (Berkeley: University of California Press, 1978), pp. 82, 174, 181.

6

On the Difference between Prevailing and Enduring

ALEXANDER WELSH

T HE terms of my title were favorites of William Faulkner's, as well as the sum and substance of his Nobel Prize speech of 1950. As I hope to show, they also correlate with the distinction between two kinds of heroism drawn by Erik H. Erikson in his Jefferson Lectures of 1973. We may be struck immediately by the common sentiments linking the name of a fictional place – Jefferson, Mississippi – that has become legendary in American culture with a distinguished series of lectures in the humanities designed to become a national institution. Furthermore, the European-born Erikson has been one of the most persuasive observers of native and other American lives. His respect for tribal communities within the larger society has been like Faulkner's, and his principal subject of study, personal identity, is the same that the novelist claimed to have explored in *Light in August.*

In the Jefferson Lectures, Erikson summarizes his findings about identity in the broadest possible terms. Personal identity is, of course, supported by the kinds of behavior that the community holds up to admiration. Two ideals of heroism, in effect, fend against the dread of having "lived the wrong life or not really lived at all" – disasters worse than death for even quite ordinary people. The first ideal is apparently more common, or more variously represented, in monuments or histories:

> Human communities, whether they consist of a tribe set in a segment of nature, or of a national empire spanning the territory and the loyalties of a variety of peoples, must attempt to reinforce that sense of identity which promises a meaning for the cycle of life within a world view more real than the certainty of death. Paradoxically speaking, however, to share such a transient sense of being

indestructible, all participants must accept a ritual code of mortality and immortality which (whether it promises a rebirth on earth or in heaven) includes the privilege and the duty, if need be, to die a heroic, or at any rate a shared death, while also being willing and eager to kill or help kill those on "the other side" who share (and live and kill and die for) another world view. The motto of this immortality, whether in combat or competition, can be said to be "kill and survive."

Instances of such heroism are found most readily in the military sphere but may also be found – as the word "competition" allows – in an agricultural, industrial, or commercial sphere. Only after he has come this far does Erikson indicate that there is a second and passive heroism that contrasts with the first kind:

> But there is the other, the transcendent, effort at insuring salvation through a conscious acceptance of finiteness. It emphasizes nothingness instead of an insistence on somebodyness. It is "not of this world," and instead of a competition for the world's goods (including those securing the earthly identity) it seeks human brotherhood in self-denial. It courts death or, at any rate, self-denial as a step toward a more real and everlasting life. It prefers self-sacrifice to killing. And it visualizes the men and women who can make this aspect of existence convincing, not as great and immortal, but as saintly and partaking of an eternal life. . . . The motto of this world view could be said to be "die and become."

Such a sweeping dichotomy, unlimited by any historical perspective other than the "human," is problematic in itself and at first glance seems only remotely useful for categorizing the themes of *Light in August*. The first sort of heroism Faulkner treats, in one way or another, in nearly all of his writings. It is the second, explicitly associated with "great religious leaders," that is more troublesome to locate in a modernist and novelistic context, even if Erikson is right to conclude that "the readiness for both extremes, that is, for a defined identity in space and time and a transcendent one is given in all human beings."[1]

But of course, *Light in August* is precisely the novel that has as its principal hero a character named Christmas, who has supported a considerable weight of exegesis as a so-called Christ figure. As a killer, Joe Christmas relates far more obviously to the first kind of heroism delineated by Erikson. Every killer gains the attention, at least, of those who do not kill. There is no more palpable power than that of taking life, and therefore a killer, no matter how depraved, enjoys a certain terrified respect from the community. Most of us will still be inclined to ask, with one of Faulkner's questioners at the University of Virginia, "Well, I was just wondering why [for] such a sort of bad man as Joe Christmas you would use Christ . . ." Faulkner pointedly did not reply to this questioner directly. Instead of explaining the "Christ symbolism," he focused on the assumption that Christmas was really a bad man and posited that, because "man is the victim of himself, or his fellows, or his own nature, or his environment," he is in fact neither good nor bad:

> Now with Christmas, for instance, he didn't know what he was. He knew that he would never know what he was, and his only salvation in order to live with himself was to repudiate mankind, to live outside the human race. And he tried to do that but nobody would let him, the human race itself wouldn't let him. And I don't think he was bad, I think he was tragic. And his tragedy was that he didn't know what he was and would never know, and that to me is the most tragic condition that an individual can have – to not know who he was.[2]

The author thus only half explains his boldly defiant conception of the hero. Christmas is not Christ in that he wants to repudiate mankind; he is not Christ by virtue of being castrated: he is like Christ only in that the human race repudiates him. According to the author, his tragedy is that of a failure of identity. Moreover, in the crassest terms, the failure to know himself reduces inexorably and artlessly to his bastardy and ignorance of his parents. When asked whether Christmas was part Negro, as he believed himself to be, Faulkner returned virtually the same answer as that about the resemblance to Christ:

> I think that was his tragedy – he didn't know what he was, and so he was nothing. He deliberately evicted himself from the human race because he didn't know which he was. That was his tragedy, that to me was the tragic, central idea of the story – that he didn't know what he was, and there was no way possible in life for him to find out. Which to me is the most tragic condition a man could find himself in – not to know what he is and to know that he will never know.[3]

125

This argument elevates personal identity to the greatest psychological significance, as in the writings of Erikson, but hardly to great moral significance. Is ignorance of who one is more tragic than knowledge of who one is coupled with personal failure? More tragic, for that matter, than being shot and mutilated for being black? Faulkner in this reply defines identity merely by birth, and regardless of that history of the hero's experience that he had reconstructed with such care and imagination in the novel itself.[4] In the interview, ignorance of "what he was" coincides with ignorance of "which he was," and this "which" can only mean black or white.

Since there is such a thing as a novelist's identity over time, these discussions at the University of Virginia cannot be completely divorced from the writing of the novel twenty-five years before. The Faulkner in the classroom is the Faulkner who, younger and less famous, wrote *Light in August*. In the novel, it may be said, Joe Christmas refuses to be guided by experience. He has accumulated in the course of his life, after all, something more than black or white blood; he has been initiated and betrayed enough in the ways of the world; he has suffered from the predictable and unpredictable actions of many different kinds of people; and he has been offered by Joanna Burden, whatever her motives, a possible future connected with the welfare, however narrowly defined, of blacks in the South. But for the purposes of this novel, the author has chosen a hero who cannot or will not profit from experience. At the very least, Faulkner portrays a man who from his earliest days is so constituted as to be unable to accept love or pity, who can even refuse food when he suspects that he is an object of kindness. Such bitterness is quite possible for a child whose injuries have resulted in self-pity so overwhelming that no consideration from others is palatable to him, but Faulkner does not pursue the psychology so far as to explain why the child would never grow up: he is satisfied with the notional inevitability of this hero's deprivation of identity. Though Christmas is sexually active and physically potent in every other respect, he does not even get anyone pregnant and continue himself by that means. Compare the ease with which a cowardly Lucas Burch replenishes the earth by fertilizing Lena Grove.

The historical Jesus did not have children that we know of, but Jesus did not kill anyone either. Both in writing *Light in August* and in talking about it, Faulkner conceives of the hero as a victim who is also a killer. The irony of calling him "Christmas" is tactical to begin with: it deliberately sets the hero apart from his fellow beings in the novel and equally – with its ironic insistence – from Jesus and the self-denial of transcendent heroism. The orphan of the novel is "nothing," but still of this world; he suffers, but fights back in his inchoate, adolescent way. When he strikes out, and above all when he kills, he recoups an identity associated with the first kind of heroism. He takes life and thereby acknowledges that life may be taken from him. When he courts death at the end, by bolting from his captors, he does not sacrifice himself for any political *or* transcendent belief. He merely completes the demonstration he has begun by striking out. All in all, Joe Christmas's way of finding himself is a way of terminating himself: but so it is, the novel suggests, with Erikson's two kinds of heroism, which are alike in assimilating death to life. Both kinds of heroism reconcile heroes and their celebrants to death; both also "court" death and, when they court it successfully, bring it on. Byron Bunch reflects that the name of the hero may serve as an "augur" or "warning" of what is to come, "if other men can only read the meaning in time" (29). At this level the irony of "Christmas" is prophetic; it suggests that the heroism of dying and becoming no longer obtains in the modern world. Faulkner's rough beast, supposedly part black, slouches from Bethlehem to an orphanage for whites, thence to farms and cities and to Jefferson, U.S.A.

Implicit in the discrimination of two kinds of heroism is a contrast between classical and Christian culture. The exchange of somebodyness (to use Erikson's term) for death in battle harks back to the archaic Greek world recalled in epic by Homer and Virgil, and to historical novels by Scott and Tolstoy. Partly because of its embodiment in epic and novel, the ideal has remained accessible to the culture in its most studied and critical forms. The ironies of killing and surviving (and surely the epic version of this heroism conveys anguish and futility that Erikson does not account for), as well as the later contrast of this ideal with dying and becoming (a still more problematic business), were already available in a literary tradition that foreshadowed and awaited Faulkner's modernist redaction. In *Light in August,* the sternly Christian McEachern calls the hero's name "heathenish" and a "sacrilege" (135), as if it logically could be both. In so responding to "Christmas," McEachern is vainly countering the novelist's tactical and prophetic moves, which have laminated the Christian to the pagan type. As Faulkner affirmed in explaining his title, this novel strives to recapture a classical and specifically Greek atmosphere or medium. For a few days in August, he explained, the light in Mississippi has "a lambence, a luminous quality . . . as though it came not from just today but from back in the old classic times." The title to him was just "a pleasant evocative title because it reminded me of that time, of a luminosity older than our Christian civilization. . . . And that was all it meant, just that luminous lambent quality of an older light than ours."[5] Such disarming understatement gives us pause, and the more we think about it the more directly "an older light than ours" appears to criticize an opposing Christian inheritance. We recall that the unmistakably true-to-type Christians of the novel – of a peculiarly Calvinist stamp, to be sure – are McEachern and Doc Hines, two oppressive adoptive fathers of a fatherless hero. And if there is an aggressive counterthrust behind the classical ambience of *Light in August,* it is in deliberately naming the hero Joe Christmas and molding him in the type of a killer – an ironic version of that hero who (in Erikson's phrase) wrests his fame from "a ritual code of mortality and immortality." In replying to the question about Christ symbolism, Faulkner assured his listeners that there was "no deliberate attempt to repeat" the story of Christ in the novel; at the same time, "Everyone that has had the story of Christ and the Passion as a part of his Christian background will in time draw from that."[6] The author acknowledges the Christian culture as his own, and in that case the deliberate crossing of heroic name and type would seem to be some sort of check or defiance of that culture.

For the next step in my argument, I need to focus on the kind of modern heroism – not yet modernist – that "prefers self-sacrifice to killing." In his Jefferson Lectures, Erikson is not concerned with the history of the novel or of political theory as such, but in both these areas he would have to take into account a secularization of the second kind of heroism and source of identity since the Enlightenment – a secularization so thorough that the "transcendent" and "eternal" aims of such heroism, let alone its "saintly" inspiration, have become hardly recognizable. Since the eighteenth century, at least, the heroism that confirms self-denial as a "way of identity" has generally reasserted itself in social and sometimes statist terms. An identity associated with self-denial and sacrifice is manifest in theories of the social contract from Hobbes to Freud; it is manifest as well in novels that teach the dependence of society on each individual's surrender of some original freedom or well-being. For the novel it is only necessary to instance Scott, the single most influential novelist of his time and, indeed, of the entire nineteenth century. Whether or not Erikson is familiar with Scott is beside the point: Faulkner certainly read some of the novels as a boy, and he is one of the few modernists to preserve in his writings substantial elements of the tradition that Scott represents.[7]

Invoking the example of Scott is always risky, because so few contemporaries have read him – though there may be less cause for anxiety on this account in writing of classic American novels than of any others. Richard Chase, who described *Light in August* as "a classic example of what is meant by speaking of an American novel as distinguished from a European one," scarcely seems acquainted with the Waverley Novels, yet the genre of "romance" that he elaborates and the statements of William Gilmore Simms and of Mark Twain that he quotes all serve to place the American novel squarely in the tradition of Scott.[8] The importance of this tradition for the present argument is that Scott regularly juxtaposed in his novels examples of both kinds of heroism, that of competition and killing being set against that of self-denial and sacrifice. The former provided much of the impetus of the action but was closely confined by the plot. In Scott's novels the effective use of force, the seizing of power and slaying of enemies, typically occurs in the past. Somebodyness (again to invoke Erikson's term) once involved the hacking and hewing of bodies and was itself confirmed by such activity. There was a time in which history, as well as personal fortunes, depended openly upon aggression. But after a certain point – conveniently symbolized in British mythography by the Glorious Revolution of 1688 – history is pacific. Henceforth violence must be criminal or futile, or both – though certain flurries of activity such as the Stuart rebellions of the eighteenth century may be seen in the Waverley Novels as romantic reenactments of the old heroism. By comparison the newer social commitment hardly seems heroic at all. A social contract requires self-denial and sacrifice at large and thereby disperses the second kind of heroism rather widely. Scott constructs his novels with particular care around the passive adventures of a representative modern hero, a young gentleman whose future accords with his respect for law and property. This hero of society witnesses the often noble gestures of the older heroism and frequently absorbs lessons of compassion as well as prudence from the action, but from now on history caters to passive rather than active heroism.

A similar restriction of constructive violence to the past is apparent in Faulkner's fiction. Colonel Sutpen in *Absalom, Absalom!* is the most imposing example of such violence, and he is viewed with a mixture of horror and admiration by Quentin Compson in the twentieth century – which is perforce the perspective of the novelist and his readers. Sutpen can at least strive to create an estate and a chance of futurity. Though Christmas belongs to the same general type, the most he can wrest from his modern world is the identity of a killer that has subsisted since primitive times. Most of the differences between Scott's and Faulkner's representations of such heroes can be elucidated in terms of Northrop Frye's historical criticism: the early-nineteenth-century novelist writes in the low mimetic mode, with gestures toward the high mimetic associated with an earlier era; the twentieth-century novelist retains the low mimetic mode and the gestures, but mainly as a kind of staging, or departure point, for prolonged descents into the ironic and circlings back to the mythic mode. Differences equally striking appear in their characterizations of the second kind of hero. Scott's passive heroes sacrifice only the freedom to take life or to act on their own behalf, and they are rewarded with marriage and ample real estate to ensure their future and the future of those who live after them. Faulkner's Quentin, in *The Sound and the Fury*, sacrifices his life altogether. His Hightower, in *Light in Au-*

gust, is a grotesque version of the passive hero, who has failed in marriage, given away his paltry estate, and become simply and rather meanly the observer that David Daiches has claimed to be the role of the hero in Scott.[9]

Readers of *Light in August* are forced to accept both the marginality of Gail Hightower's existence in Jefferson – a marginality insisted on throughout – and the centrality of the same figure to the design of the novel – a centrality more evident at the end. This odd contradiction was already implicit in Scott's novels and in countless European and American novels modeled upon them, but in Faulkner's handling both the authorial presence and the hero's role in the action have partly disintegrated. Scott may be thought to stand personally closer to some of his passive heroes (Waverley, Osbaldistone, Latimer) than to others; these heroes are marginal only in the sense that they do not propel the action, which nevertheless surrounds them and endows them with the future. The author portrays the whole affair with assumed objectivity but centrally endorses the fable of property and history throughout. In *Light in August* – to take up the authorial contradiction first – Faulkner stands outside his characters and the several actions: the constantly shifting point of view is enough to assure objectivity of a sort. Yet he involves himself subjectively in *Light in August* much more than Scott does in any of his novels, and for the denouement he is present in at least three of the characters. Percy Grimm and Gavin Stevens he introduces only at the end, to bring the action to a stop: though Faulkner later distinctly disavowed his connection to both characters, they have, respectively, the authorial roles of driving the action to its conclusion and commenting upon it.[10] Much more marvelously and carefully wrought, objectively and subjectively, is Hightower, before whom the final action unfolds without his willing it. Hightower is the main vehicle for entry into this novel by the author and many readers, but at the same time his objective portrayal results in a grotesque. He is not only old and flabby and cuckolded, he is so marginal as to be tolerated by his neighbors in Jefferson only in the way in which, anthropologists tell us, communities tolerate certain persons as shameless ones. Faulkner's outsider-insider instances wonderfully

131

the crux of authorial presence and precludes the attachment of all but tolerant readers. It is with a last triumph of Hightower's consciousness, then, that *Light in August* essentially closes:

> It is as though they had merely waited until he could find something to pant with, to be reaffirmed in triumph and desire with, with this last left of honor and pride and life. He hears above his heart the thunder increase, myriad and drumming. Like a long sighing of wind in trees it begins, then they sweep into sight, borne now upon a cloud of phantom dust. They rush past, forwardleaning in the saddles, with brandished arms, beneath whipping ribbons from slanted and eager lances; with tumult and soundless yelling they sweep past like a tide whose crest is jagged with the wild heads of horses and the brandished arms of men like the crater of the world in explosion. They rush past, are gone; the dust swirls skyward sucking, fades away into the night which has fully come. Yet leaning forward in the window, his bandaged head huge and without depth upon the twin blobs of his hands upon the ledge, it seems to him that he still hears them: the wild bugles and the clashing sabres and the dying thunder of hooves. (pp. 466–7)

After this crescendo – of which these are only the final measures – the light-hearted coda that accompanies Lena Grove and Byron Bunch out of town counts for little that touches Faulkner or his readers personally. But note that the treatment of Hightower is grotesque to the end: his huge head and blobs of hands, "leaning forward in the window" contrasted to "forwardleaning in the saddles," and finally the dying echoes of a poet, Tennyson, whom the character himself does not altogether respect.

From the perspective of literary history, Hightower interests us because, in his original profession of minister of the gospel, he connects the passive heroism of secular fiction to the second heroism described by Erikson. Just as Christmas, one who kills, poses a painfully ironic challenge to heroism of the religious sort, Hightower is its parodic similitude. Indeed, in that final narrative of his consciousness he is still dying and becoming, as Erikson puts it. Hightower has meanwhile been secularized in the course of his own personal history, through his obsession with his mortal and immortal grandfather and as a result of the action of his congregation against him. A defrocked minister, he hears the church music from outside the church:

132

Listening, he seems to hear within it the apotheosis of his own history, his own land, his own environed blood: that people from which he sprang and among whom he lives who can never take either pleasure or catastrophe or escape from either, without brawling over it. Pleasure, ecstasy, they cannot seem to bear: their escape from it is in violence, in drinking and fighting and praying; catastrophe too, the violence identical and apparently inescapable *And so why should not their religion drive them to crucifixion of themselves and one another?* he thinks. (p. 347)

Though he thinks now about *"their"* religion he remains sufficiently a minister to judge the community as moving away from what Erikson calls "human brotherhood in self-denial." Again, the conception of Hightower points to the very absence of that faith in society that Scott implicitly relied upon. Like Scott's heroes, Hightower is a witness to violence round about him; but whereas in the Waverley Novels (as for a time in *Absalom, Absalom!*) violence may have achieved something in the past, in *Light in August* it is a symptom of personal escape and social exhaustion. Hightower the character leads a more subjective life than any dreamed of by Scott's characters. The violence that he witnesses over and over again is not the brutal death of Joe Christmas his contemporary but the death of his grandfather, foraging in Jefferson at the end of the Civil War. And that death is itself absurd. The grandfather is a class-one Eriksonian hero who has killed men – so Hightower has been told and believes – "by the hundreds" (452), yet he was shot down while attempting to steal chickens:

This is beautiful. Listen. Try to see it. Here is that fine shape of eternal youth and virginal desire which makes heroes. . . . You see before the crash, in the abrupt red glare the horses with wide eyes and nostrils in tossing heads, sweatstained; the gleam of metal, the white gaunt faces of living scarecrows who have not eaten all they wanted at one time since they could remember; perhaps some of them had already dismounted, perhaps one or two had already entered the henhouse. All this you see before the crash of the shotgun comes: then blackness again. It was just the one shot. (pp. 458–9)

The rhetoric – most of which I have had to omit – has a paradoxical effect: it persuades us momentarily of the heroism of those days and the sad mockery of that death; but since it flows, ceaselessly and insistently, from Hightower's obsession with the event, the more assent it claims from the reader, the less it wins. Because of the gallant exaggeration, both the action and the witnessing are reduced to "desire," though the double futility of the character and of the past by which he is held somehow does not prevent him from commenting intelligently on present-day Jefferson.

Much has been made by the best critics of Faulkner, most notably by Cleanth Brooks, of the sense in which Hightower rejoins the community that is Jefferson at the end of the novel.[11] Because of his ousting from his church, the minister believes he has "bought immunity" (293), and now he is drawn back into the community by witnessing Christmas's death and assisting with the birth of Lena Grove's child. These are, however, very minimal actions. His belated effort to save Christmas is as useless as it is feeble, and considering everything we are made to understand about Grove, it is hard to believe that she would not have given birth to a healthy child without assistance. Moreover, the community is subject to a good deal more criticism in *Light in August* than Brooks allows. The community comes alive, just as it does in *Oliver Twist*, when there is a fire to watch and a murderer to be hunted down. (In Dickens's novel, the murderer Sikes actually assists in putting out the fire.) Faulkner's satire of the inhabitants of Jefferson – and, by extension, of the citizens of most towns – is acute and reflective, and since he goes out of his way to make some of his comments, he presumably meant them. This is not Hightower's voice but that of a narrator unnamed:

> So they moiled and clotted, believing that the flames, the blood, the body that had died three years ago and had just now begun to live again, cried out for vengeance, not believing that the rapt infury of the flames and the immobility of the body were both affirmations of an attained bourne beyond the hurt and harm of man. Not that. Because the other made nice believing. Better than the shelves and the counters filled with longfamiliar objects bought, not because the owner desired them or admired them, could take any pleasure in the owning of them, but in order to cajole or trick other men into buying them at a profit; and who must now and then contemplate both the objects which had not yet sold and the men who could buy them but had not yet done so, with anger and maybe outrage and maybe despair too. Better than the musty offices where the lawyers

waited lurking among ghosts of old lusts and lies, or where doctors waited with sharp knives and sharp drugs, telling man, believing that he should believe, without resorting to printed admonishments, that they labored for that end whose ultimate attainment would leave them with nothing whatever to do. (p. 273)

Of course, such satire appeals to a standard not always expressed but implicit in the judgment of the satirist and shared by someone. The community that Brooks celebrates in Faulkner's fiction is often simply this implied background of values against which both contemptible existences and cruel actions may be seen for what they are.

In considering the need for personal identity that calls upon and even helps to create differing kinds of heroism, we have to see that sheer ongoing human existence, if not beside the point, belongs to another category of action altogether. That there must be such ongoing existence, sexually generated, no one would deny, but the heroic life usually defines itself against it, and literature has accordingly established certain conventions for representing it apart. Shakespeare, capitalizing on native English drama, employed for this purpose a contrast of high and low styles. Indeed, *Henry IV*, which seems to have been the play of Shakespeare's foremost in Faulkner's mind while writing *Light in August*, is perhaps the most famous instance of the procedure: the wagoners and ostlers, soldiers and tapsters, thieves and prostitutes in the play represent an ongoing life that persists from generation to generation regardless of dynastic change. With marked economy Shakespeare can thus include a range of human activity apart from the conflict of heroes, and the study of heroism, in his historical drama. The low characters establish the depth of community, if you will, without which the high could not live – without which history would not go on. Again, it was Scott who, with similar effect, adopted and reinvigorated the contrast of styles for the novel. In his best novels, such as *Old Mortality*, revolutionary changes in the political history of the nation and conflicting heroic ideals leave the ongoing life of the low characters – some of whom have been involved in the action and some of whom have managed to evade it – more or less untouched. As in Shakespeare, the difference of high and low is literally rendered by style. The principal persons perform serious actions and speak standard English; the folk engage in comic byplay and speak the local dialect. This precedent was exploited in the nineteenth century by novelists as different as Dickens and George Eliot, and the convention was used with powerful effect by Hardy and Faulkner. In his excellent study of *Light in August*, François Pitavy confesses some puzzlement with two dialect characters, Byron Bunch and Lena Grove, in the chapter that concludes the novel. The one is "puppetlike at the end," he remarks, and the other "bovine as ever." He finds it "ironic that the characters possessed of admirable qualities should leave a comic impression."[12] But if the French critic would think more specifically of literature in English, the conception of these two characters would strike him as much more conventional. The character named Joe Christmas is every bit as low on the social scale as they are, but he has been generated from the ironic thrust of modernism and is a type of the hero, which they are not. Faulkner concludes with Bunch and Grove in order to restore the sense of ongoing life in the frame of his narrative, but their behavior is something of a joke from any heroic perspective.

In my judgment, Brooks confuses the picture by involving Lena Grove so unreservedly in his notion of community. To be sure, Grove attracts the human sympathy of such as the Armstids and Bunch, but "she *is* nature," in Brooks's words: in one sentence he subsequently links "her instinct for nature" with "her rapport with the community."[13] She cannot represent both nature and the community – unless, indeed, that community is construed as biological rather than social. Faulkner does not help by speaking of Lena Grove in 1955 as if she had heroic stature: "It didn't really matter to her in her destiny whether her man was Lucas Burch or not. It was her destiny to have a husband and children and she knew it, and so she went out and attended to it without asking help from anyone."[14] The novel, however, rather slyly plays on the woman's pretensions, and the reason she does not ask for help is that she does not think it ladylike. For the most part, except for a page or two devoted to her childhood, Grove exists below the level of consciousness. The narrative of her inner life closes with her arrival at womanhood, an event neatly registered by a double entendre: "She had not opened it [the window] a dozen times hardly before she discovered that she should not have opened it at all. She said to herself, 'That's just my luck'" (3). The so-called destiny that begins with a sexual joke disappears from view with another such joke aimed at Bunch in the final chapter: "Why, Mr Bunch. Aint you ashamed. You might have woke the baby, too" (477) – a line that so tickled the author that he could quote it from memory.[15] These two are intrinsically and traditionally low characters, and in this important conventional sense they are anti-heroic. Inevitably they stand as a rebuke and a check to the heroic, whether the kind represented by Christmas or by Hightower (Grove's pregnancy versus Christmas's murderousness, Bunch's compassion versus Hightower's withdrawal). But this potential critique of the heroic is never developed to the extraordinary extent that it is by Shakespeare (Falstaff versus all in *Henry IV*) or indeed by Scott (the impertinence of Mause Headrigg, Andrew Fairservice, Caleb Balderston). On the contrary, the author of *Light in August* identifies with both heroic perspectives and may look down upon his other characters.[16]

The word "survive" was perhaps an unfortunate choice in the motto "kill and survive" that Erikson suggests for the first kind of heroism. The context makes perfectly clear that by "survive" Erikson means survival in the memory of others, the immortality of "a ritual code of mortality and immortality." The Lena Groves and Byron Bunches do not survive in that sense, though they do walk out of the novel on their feet. Their counterparts in real life survive only in the sense that others like them will get and bear children, climb in and out of wagons, work in planing mills, and have relatively little to say for themselves. They are not heroes to emulate, nor is personal identity so much at stake for them – that is the point of the joke in the novel about the child's father and the scarcely discernible typographical difference between "Bunch" and "Burch." Remember that Joe Christmas is a bastard of the same class and indifferent making as the child of Lena Grove and Lucas Burch. But he is not a "low" character within the convention I have referred to, and there would be no danger of confusing him with the type if he were not a hero in the ironic mode. An index of Faulkner's success with *Light in August* is that Christmas does indeed kill and survive in the sense that Erikson intended: so much so that many persons who have never read the novel have undoubtedly heard of him and would be able to say something about his fate. Such is the fame, or destiny, of heroes who kill and are killed, especially when a novelist has the effrontery to give one of them a name redolent of a different heroism.

Having traced Erikson's two kinds of heroism in the secular tradition of the novel and having tentatively established that Christmas and Hightower, notwithstanding the name of the first and the obsession of the second, belong respectively to these two types, we are now in a position to ask in what way this difference is confirmed or denied by Faulkner's Nobel Prize speech. Brief as it is, that is by no means an easy speech to unravel. Certain substantives – "love and honor and pity and pride and compassion and sacrifice" – Faulkner simply asserts to be "truths" without forming any propositions about them that would enable the audience to dispute the point. Then he seems to be saying several things at once about enduring and prevailing, which he does not elaborate upon as concepts but first contrasts, employing strictly intransitive verbs in the future indicative, and finally conjoins as infinitives.

Here are the sentences that play upon these two verbs and bring the Nobel Prize speech to a close:

> It is easy enough to say that man is immortal simply because he will endure: that when the last ding-dong of doom has clanged and faded from the last worthless rock hanging tideless in the last red and dying evening, that even then there will still be one more sound: that of his puny inexhaustible voice, still talking. I refuse to accept this. I believe that man will not merely endure: he will prevail. He is immortal, not because he alone among creatures has an inexhaustible voice, but because he has a soul, a spirit capable of compassion and sacrifice and endurance. The poet's, the writer's, duty is to write about these things. It is his privilege to help man endure by lifting his heart, by reminding him of the courage and honor and hope and pride and compassion and pity and sacrifice which have been the glory of his past. The poet's voice need not merely be the record of man, it can be one of the props, the pillars to help him endure and prevail.[17]

Among other things, Faulkner is casting his lot against modernism in its more consistent forms – the inexhaustible voices of the ironic mode as practiced by Samuel Beckett, for example. That his subject is a restoration of heroism is confirmed by the rallying cry and by the traditional role assigned to the poet, singing the glories of the past as props to the present. In short, if we can understand what Faulkner is talking about, so could the people of Scott's time or of Homer's. At first he makes a point similar to the one I have just made with respect to his own characters Grove and Bunch: that enduring is not the activity that makes one immortal and that, by implication, he who is immortal will have prevailed rather than merely endured. As soon as this difference is asserted, however, the speaker seems willing to extend a helping hand to endurance, for the next two times he utters the word, as noun and verb, he is no longer boldly dismissive but warmly inclusive of the lesser effort. Finally, two verbs conclude the famous speech in simple conjunction, "endure and prevail." So it seems as if Faulkner strove to enforce a distinction – "I believe that man will not merely endure: he will prevail" – that he finally could not sustain.

Let us suppose, alternatively, that the distinction Faulkner strives to make good is not that between heroic and less than heroic existence, as in the contrast of styles that he exploits in his novels, but rather one between the two kinds of heroism that he exploits in Christmas and Hightower. If we proceed to map Faulkner's Nobel Prize speech upon Erikson's Jefferson Lectures, "prevail" would have to refer to the first kind of heroism, whose motto is "kill and survive," and "endure" would have to refer to the second kind, whose motto is "die and become." Only the transcendent gesture of "become," for the second kind of heroism, causes much difficulty in this mapping, and that difficulty is lessened if we regard more narrowly the post-Enlightenment and novelistic version of passive heroism (though to invoke the social contract may be to exchange one mystery for another). What then can "prevail" denote that is not already expressed by "endure"? The answer would appear to be victory, the overcoming of the enemy. In a military context – strongly hinted at by the epic role designed for the poet – the difference between prevailing and enduring corresponds to that between successful offensive and defensive actions. But victory over what or whom? Offense always raises more sharply than defense the question of the enemy. Whom to kill, what to overcome? This uncertainty, I suggest, is one reason that the determination on victory in the fifth sentence from the end of the speech gives way to the far less ambitious conjunction of "endure and prevail" in the last sentence. The other reason is that Faulkner no sooner insists, at his boldest, that there is a difference between prevailing and enduring than he confuses them, for in the fourth sentence from the end he associates prevailing with "a spirit capable of compassion and sacrifice and endurance." That confusion, whether deliberate or otherwise, seems to say once again that any heroism will do, the point being that mere existence will not do.

For some readers of *Light in August,* such questions are no more resolved in the novel than they are in the speech. Alfred Kazin, for example, criticizes "Faulkner's reckless, desperate eagerness to wrest all the possible implications from his material, to think it out interminably, since there is no end to all one's possible meditations round and round the human cycle," and he comes down hard on the novelist's "attempt to will his painful material into a kind of harmony it does not really possess."[18] Pitavy, on the other hand, recognizes in the novel roughly two kinds of heroism and identities based upon them. For him *Light in August* is about "the ways by which a man may affirm his existence: he may choose revolt and solitude, both sterile and deadly, yet consonant with human dignity, or he may choose acceptance, responsibility, and solidarity."[19] Pitavy, however, includes Lena Grove on a par with Christmas and Hightower in this assessment. Moreover, he adopts the novel's negative judgment of Christmas ("sterile and deadly") without stopping to recall anything negative or strange or amusing about Hightower and Grove ("acceptance, responsibility, and solidarity"?). To divide the novel in these terms is to reassimilate it to the novel of the nineteenth century, to re-dress the themes of Scott in a more modern vocabulary while shunning Faulkner's deeper revisions, both his elevation of Christmas and his sympathetic derision of Hightower.

Kazin no more than indicates that, for him, the themes of the novel — its implications and meditations, as he puts it — do not fit together. Pitavy, by trying to sort out the characters and themes, may have shown us just where the imbalance lies. I have already argued that the novelist does not allow Lena Grove the wit to do more than biologically reproduce herself and that she does not occupy the same level of representation as the heroic characters, both of whom are conceived in the ironic mode. Now let me suggest how Faulkner in *Light in August* exploits the difference between prevailing and enduring, precisely by means of a relentless play on the difference between the sexes. And here my argument must return to the principal action of the novel: the murder of a woman by a man, whether black or white or uncertain of his identity.

In the ringing affirmations of his Nobel Prize speech, Faulkner does not concern himself with gender differences, but a moment's reflection may suggest how close "prevail" and "endure" come to describing age-old, traditionally approved postures of male and female humanity respectively. Erikson likewise places gender differences mainly to one side, yet the terms of his distinction – combat and competition for one kind of heroism and sacrifice and self-denial for the other – are quite as memorably male and female. This apparent congruity of heroic kinds with accepted gender characteristics goes a long way back in time – far earlier than the writing of novels or the idea of a social contract – and its origins are the subject of much serious study at present. We simply do not know as much of the history and working of such assumptions as we ought to, except that many or most of the averred characteristics of women are deeply prejudicial. Like other writers who have continuously interpreted culture for us, novelists have not all embraced the same prejudices or embraced them to the same degree. But prejudices about women are bruited about so freely in Faulkner's novels that he has frequently been put down as a misogynist.[20] Even when Faulkner speaks handsomely of women, they have reason to beware. *Light in August,* he told his audience at the University of Virginia, "began with Lena Grove, the idea of the young girl with nothing, pregnant, determined to find her sweetheart. It was – that was out of my admiration for women, for the courage and endurance of women. As I told that story I had to get more and more into it, but that was mainly the story of Lena Grove."[21] But a comparison of women in general to Lena Grove is an extremely doubtful compliment to begin with, and yoking women's "courage" to "endurance" shows that they need not expect to prevail. The character in question, to be sure, does prevail over Byron Bunch – in the old uneasy joke that pretends to give women their way.

"He will prevail" promises victory – the victory that all men and boys are supposed to want but that, not surprisingly, eludes Faulkner at the level of abstraction of the Nobel Prize speech. Victory over whom or what? The aim of prevailing is compelling for adolescents but rather a nuisance for grown men: that is the convenience of having a second sex to do the enduring, of imagining that they wish to prevail, and of putting them down. Such an arrangement is likely to be especially tempting, because virtually unchecked, in the invented action of a novel. Joe Christmas, the predominant male force in *Light in August*, engages in a more or less constant struggle with enemies who are women, except for a "brief respite" (113) that would seem to coincide with the years between infancy and adolescence that Freud called the "latency period." From the first "womanshenegro" that Joe kicks and strikes without bedding (147) to his affair with Joanna Burden, they are all enemies. Burden is by far the most complicated of these women, as well as the kindest to Christmas: what is astonishing is how readily critics have accepted what Faulkner writes of her corruption and his comparative purity, his "life of healthy and normal sin" in brothels across America (246). Just as many critics accept the limited and passionless Grove at higher than her face value, so they go along with the denigration of Burden. Much has been made – rather coyly – of the name "Burden," whereas more comment might be directed toward Faulkner's choice of "Joanna" – or the female of the species Joe. Her depiction is, among other things, a travesty of the female abolitionist lusting after Negroes.[22]

It may (or may not) be useful to ask why Christmas and Faulkner are so upset by menstruation, which seems to be the nastiest thing about the enemy. In the most elaborate of his initiations, Christmas's introduction to menstruation takes precedence over his introduction to sex with Bobbie (173–8); his last sexual affair is put an end to by Burden's menopause (99). Against these antipathies the narrative offers Lena Grove, who does not menstruate because she is pregnant – and who probably wouldn't think it ladylike. The logic would seem to be that women are all right as long as they are ready to conceive or bear children, but that conclusion may also be too hasty. "The husband of a mother, whether he be the father or not, is already a cuckold" (298). Those are the words of Hightower, which perhaps ought to be discounted, but they are confirmed independently by the way Grove later uses "we" to refer exclusively to herself and her child (470).

Hightower's mysterious saying about "good" women is still more damning of the sex. "There have been good women who were martyrs to brutes, in their cups and such. But what woman, good or bad, has ever suffered from any brute as men have suffered from good women?" (299). Women are so used to enduring that at worst they can be martyrs; men, so bound to prevail that they can really suffer. The additional fillip about good women may also be discounted as Hightower's but is confirmed independently by Christmas's experience of Mrs. McEachern and Miss Burden: "It was the woman: that soft kindness which he believed himself doomed to be forever victim of and which he hated worse than he did the hard and ruthless justice of men. 'She is trying to make me cry,' he thought" (158). And the evidence is that Christmas finally cuts Burden's throat because she makes her pity for him too plain: " 'It's because she started praying over me,' he said" (98). These relations with good women suggest that Christmas is not only a man ignorant of his identity but a man terrified of love. If so, the irony of his name is still more apparent.

The attitude toward women in the novel is not subject to logic, nor would it necessarily be a better novel if it were. Sweeping prejudices have a way of invigorating expression, and Faulkner makes it pretty clear that his prejudiced characters are just that, even when he may be using them to express his own feelings. In *Light in August* he skillfully exposes the psychology of both Hightower and Christmas. He has observed and lived alongside these characters in the process of writing the novel, and their verbal and physical attacks upon women reflect a wide spectrum of uncertainties. Faulkner's novels often absorb energy and acuteness of feeling from a kind of whipsaw of sexual anxiety and prejudice that is the author's own.[23] Nothing brings easier relief to an uncertain sense of personal identity, in real or imagined life, than letting go against the members of a different group – which may be another nation, race, or sex. Faulkner, who was freer of national and racial bias than most of his compatriots, rather enjoyed abusing women, to whom he also felt deeply subject. His sexual bias in part responded to and in part propelled the warlike theme of enduring and prevailing in his fiction.

A just reading of *Light in August* requires us to remember that Joe and Joanna *both* die very bloody deaths. In his determination to display the extremity of Joe Christmas's plight, Faulkner impugns the sexuality of Joanna Burden to the extent that her death is unlamented. He all the more easily indicts her by means of stunning generalizations about female impurity, as contrasted to the "healthy and normal sin" engaged in by his hero. He carefully arranges that she should first threaten Christmas's death and her own suicide, so that the reader may judge that the murder makes little final difference. But if the decisive action of the tragedy is to result from the hero's failure of identity, why palliate his crime with her futile aggression? In Faulkner's own reflections on the novel – "and that to me is the most tragic condition that an individual can have – to not know who he was" – he seems to be saying that his hero was pitifully incapacitated, instead of recalling that Christmas has ruthlessly decapitated a woman who has sheltered and nourished him – and sexually served him – for three years. Presumably Christmas might once more have run away at this point, but he seizes at last a fatal identity for himself by killing. All of these considerations come appropriately into the tragedy that Faulkner designs to narrate, but the tragedy is actually weakened by Burden's supposed corruption. Thus the murderer, hapless as he is, is superior to his victim. The characterization of the two, manifestly a production of sexual bias, is then uneasily confirmed by the event, for in the crudest sense, to be a murderer is to prevail, whereas to be murdered is merely to endure. Christmas is hunted and murdered in turn, so that he both prevails and endures: as in the Nobel Prize speech, Faulkner first elevates prevailing above enduring and then settles for their conjunction. But the woman he more or less discards in the process.

Faulkner's great achievement in *Light in August,* in my view, lies in the subtle modernist redaction of traditional kinds of heroism.

Not only are the two main types represented in Christmas and Hightower shrewdly investigated anew, as to how they must act under the constraints of modern social life, but their mythical significance is challenged forthrightly. From the passive but stabilizing hero of Scott and the nineteenth century has emerged an ineffectual and grotesque Hightower, whose limitations never altogether destroy or obscure from us his human feeling and judgment. From the active hero who sometimes moved history in decisive ways in the past has emerged the nearly purely destructive Christmas – though he is not, as Faulkner almost seems to believe, destructive solely of himself. By focusing attention on the fate of Christmas and the dreams of Hightower, the novelist asks what personal identity is possible for them; by writing of them within a tradition of a novel that speaks much more widely to the needs of society at large, he implicitly asks what contribution such "heroes" can any longer make. The answer is, apparently none except in spirit; and the grim sport of prevailing over women and its humorous counterpart – moral equivalents of war, so to speak – only make the answer more sad. At the same time, Faulkner's strenuous conception of a killer named Christmas reduces the Eriksonian model of two heroisms, and the venerable traditions behind them, to a single ironic courting of death. In this troubling display of the futility of the heroism that it would praise, *Light in August* is both astute and moving.

NOTES

1. Erik H. Erikson, *Dimensions of a New Identity: The 1973 Jefferson Lectures in the Humanities* (New York: Norton, 1974), pp. 42–3.
2. *Faulkner in the University: Class Conferences at the University of Virginia, 1957–1958*, ed. Frederick L. Gwynn and Joseph L. Blotner (Charlottesville: University of Virginia Press, 1959), pp. 117–18.
3. Ibid., p. 72.
4. This portion of the novel (chapters 6–12) was apparently written later than the rest; see Regina K. Fadiman, *Faulkner's "Light in August": A Description and Interpretation of the Revisions* (Charlottesville: University Press of Virginia, 1975).
5. Gwynn and Blotner, eds. *Faulkner in the University*, p. 199. "Maybe

the connection was with Lena Grove," Faulkner added. Her untrammeled sexuality, needless to say, can be viewed as pre-Christian; but I see Grove within a postclassical frame of the contrast of styles, as I explain below.

6. Ibid., p. 117.

7. "Every Southern household when they bought books they bought Scott." Faulkner speculated that the Scottish novels had a special affinity with the history of the American South and were also a very good buy. See ibid., p. 135.

8. Richard Chase, *The American Novel and Its Tradition* (London: Bell, 1958), p. 206; for Simms and Mark Twain, see pp. 16 and 146–7.

9. David Daiches, "Scott's Achievement as a Novelist," in *Literary Essays* (Edinburgh: Oliver and Boyd, 1956), p. 93.

10. Stevens's comments are "rationalizations": see Gwynn and Blotner, eds., *Faulkner in the University*, p. 72. Grimm is a "Fascist galahad": see a letter to Malcolm Cowley of 1945 in *Selected Letters of William Faulkner*, ed. Joseph Blotner (New York: Random House, 1977), p. 202.

11. Cleanth Brooks, *William Faulkner: The Yoknapatawpha Country* (New Haven, Conn.: Yale University Press, 1963), pp. 47–74.

12. François Pitavy, *Faulkner's "Light in August,"* trans. Gillian E. Cook (Bloomington: Indiana University Press, 1973), p. 118.

13. Brooks, *William Faulkner*, pp. 67, 72.

14. *Lion in the Garden: Interviews with William Faulkner 1926–1962*, ed. James B. Meriwether and Michael Millgate (New York: Random House, 1968), p. 253.

15. Ibid., p. 253.

16. This condescension is remarked on by Alfred Kazin, "The Stillness of *Light in August*" (1958), in *Faulkner: A Collection of Critical Essays*, ed. Robert Penn Warren (Englewood Cliffs, N.J.: Prentice-Hall, 1966), p. 161. Kazin includes Christmas with Grove among characters whom Faulkner tended "to generalize and to overpraise." My own reading, equally subjective, is that the novelist identified rather closely with Christmas.

17. William Faulkner, *Essays, Speeches, and Public Letters*, ed. James B. Meriwether (New York: Random House, 1966), p. 120.

18. Kazin, "The Stillness of *Light in August*," p. 148.

19. Pitavy, *Faulkner's "Light in August,"* p. 159.

20. Irving Howe puts the matter well in his *William Faulkner: A Critical Study*, 2nd ed. (New York: Vintage, 1962): "This inclination toward misogyny need not always be taken too literally or solemnly. . . . But

so persistent a devotion to popular attitudes, in both their humorous surface and earnest core, must be related to some governing personal bias, some obscure uneasiness before these victims of 'periodic filth' " (excerpted in Warren, ed., *Faulkner*, p. 283). A sensitive and understated guide to the personal elements in the work is David Minter, *William Faulkner: His Life and Work* (Baltimore: Johns Hopkins University Press, 1980).

21. Gwynn and Blotner, eds., *Faulkner in the University*, p. 74. Some feminists would argue that this language for creativity – "I had to get more and more into it" – is too blatantly and exclusively masculine.

22. The character and name are distantly linked to Jo-Addie in the early attempt at novel writing called "Elmer," hence also to Addie Bundren of *As I Lay Dying* and what may be thought of as the maternal undergrowth of Faulkner's fiction. For an account of "Elmer," see Minter, *William Faulkner*, pp. 55–64.

23. Albert J. Guerard has described the contribution of Faulkner's misogyny to his art, with particular reference to *Sanctuary*; see *The Triumph of the Novel: Dickens, Dostoevsky, Faulkner* (New York: Oxford University Press, 1976), pp. 109–35.

Notes on Contributors

André Bleikasten, Professor of American Literature at the Université de Strasbourg, is the author of *Faulkner's "As I Lay Dying"* (1973), *The Most Splendid Failure: Faulkner's "The Sound and the Fury"* (1976), and *Parcours de Faulkner* (1982).

Martin Kreiswirth, Associate Professor of English at the University of Western Ontario, is the author of *William Faulkner: The Making of a Novelist* (1983) and of essays on British and American literature.

Michael Millgate, Professor of English at the University of Toronto, is the author of *William Faulkner* (1961) and *The Achievement of William Faulkner* (1966) and coeditor of *Lion in the Garden: Interviews with William Faulkner 1926–1962* (1968).

Alexander Welsh, Professor of English at the University of California, Los Angeles, is the author of major studies of Scott and Dickens and, more recently, of *Reflections on the Hero as Quixote* (1981) and *George Eliot and Blackmail* (1985).

Judith Bryant Wittenberg, Associate Professor of English at Simmons College, is the author of *Faulkner: The Transfiguration of Biography* (1979) and of essays on Faulkner and other American and British writers.

Selected Bibliography

The text of *Light in August* accepted as standard for the purposes of this volume is that of the first edition (New York: Harrison Smith and Robert Haas, 1932), which has been, and remains, widely available in many forms. Subsequent reissues of this edition include the following: London: Chatto & Windus, 1933; New York: Random House, 1940; New York: New Directions, 1967; New York: Random House, 1967; New York: Modern Library, 1967 (Modern Library College Editions paperback, with an introduction by Cleanth Brooks); New York: Vintage Books, 1972 (paperback). [See James B. Meriwether, "The Books of William Faulkner," *Mississippi Quarterly* 35 (Summer 1982):270–1.]

Comprehensive listings of Faulkner criticism and scholarship can be found in Thomas L. McHaney, *William Faulkner: A Reference Guide* (Boston: G. K. Hall, 1976), and in John Bassett's *William Faulkner: An Annotated Checklist of Criticism* (New York: David Lewis, 1972) and *Faulkner: An Annotated Checklist of Recent Criticism* (Kent, Ohio: Kent State University Press, 1983). The excellent analytical survey by James B. Meriwether in *Sixteen Modern American Authors: A Survey of Research and Criticism*, ed. Jackson R. Bryer (New York: Norton, 1973), can be supplemented by the annual reviews in *American Literary Scholarship* (Modern Language Association of America) and the summer issues of *Mississippi Quarterly*.

The list below consists primarily of books and articles of fairly recent date. Earlier studies well worth consulting have been mentioned in the introduction to this volume, and the following works in particular may be regarded as being of continuing importance: Cleanth Brooks, *William Faulkner: The Yoknapatawpha Country* (New Haven, Conn.: Yale University Press, 1963); Michael Millgate, *The Achievement of William Faulkner* (London: Constable, 1966); François L. Pitavy, *Faulkner's "Light in August"* (Bloomington: Indiana University Press, 1973); and Olga L. Vickery, *The Novels of William Faulkner* (Baton Rouge: Louisiana State University press, 1959; rev. ed., 1964). Edmond L. Volpe's chapter on the novel in *A Reader's Guide to William Faulkner* (New York: Farrar, Straus, 1964) will also be found useful, as will the following anthologies: David L. Minter, ed., *Twentieth Century Interpretations of "Light in August": A Collection of Critical Essays* (Englewood Cliffs, N.J.: Prentice-Hall, 1969); M. Thomas Inge, ed., *The Merrill Studies in "Light in August"* (Columbus, Ohio: Charles E. Merrill, 1971); John B. Vickery and Olga W. Vickery, eds., *"Light in August" and the Critical Spectrum* (Belmont, Calif.: Wadsworth, 1971); and especially François L. Pitavy, ed., *William Faulkner's "Light in August": A Critical Casebook* (New York: Garland Publishing, 1982).

Adamowski, T. H. "Joe Christmas: The Tyranny of Childhood." *Novel* 4 (Spring 1971):240–51.

Bleikasten, André. "Fathers in Faulkner." In *The Fictional Father: Lacanian Readings of the Text,* ed. Robert Con Davis. Amherst: University of Massachusetts Press, 1981, pp. 115–46.

Parcours de Faulkner. Paris: Editions Ophrys, 1982.

Burroughs, Franklin G., Jr. "God the Father and Motherless Children: *Light in August.*" *Twentieth Century Literature* 19 (July 1973):189–202.

Collins, R. G. "*Light in August:* Faulkner's Stained Glass Triptych." *Mosaic* 7 (Fall 1973):97–157.

Davis, Thadious M. *Faulkner's Negro: Art and the Southern Context.* Baton Rouge: Louisiana State University Press, 1982.

Fowler, Doreen. "Faulkner's *Light in August:* A Novel in Black and White." *Arizona Quarterly* 40 (Winter 1984):305–24.

Gresset, Michel. *Faulkner ou la fascination.* Paris: Klincksieck, 1982.

Howe, Irving. *William Faulkner: A Critical Study.* First pub. 1952; 3rd ed., revised, Chicago: University of Chicago Press, 1975.

Hungerford, Harold. "Past and Present in *Light in August.*" *American Literature* 55 (May 1983):183–98.

Jenkins, Lee Clinton. *Faulkner and Black-White Relations: A Psychoanalytical Approach.* New York: Columbia University Press, 1981.

Kartiganer, Donald M. *The Fragile Thread: The Meaning of Form in Faulkner's Novels.* Amherst: University of Massachusetts Press, 1979.

Korenman, Joan S. "Faulkner's Grecian Urn." *Southern Literary Journal* 7 (Fall 1974):3–23.

Lind, Ilse Dusoir. "Faulkner's Uses of Poetic Drama." In *Faulkner, Modernism, and Film: Faulkner and Yoknapatawpha, 1978,* ed. Evans Harrington and Ann J. Abadie. Jackson: University Press of Mississippi, 1979, pp. 66–81.

Meats, Stephen E. "The Chronology of *Light in August.*" In *The Novels of William Faulkner: "Light in August,"* ed. François Pitavy. New York: Garland Publishing, 1982, pp. 227–35.

Nash, H. C. "Faulkner's 'Furniture Repairer and Dealer': Knitting up *Light in August.*" *Modern Fiction Studies* 16 (Winter 1970–1):529–31.

Reed, Joseph W., Jr. *Faulkner's Narrative.* New Haven, Conn.: Yale University Press, 1973.

Ruppersburg, Hugh M. *Voice and Eye in Faulkner's Fiction.* Athens: University of Georgia Press, 1983.

Taylor, Carole Anne. "*Light in August:* The Epistemology of Tragic Paradox." *Texas Studies in Literature and Language* 22 (Spring 1980):48–68.

Tucker, John. "William Faulkner's *Light in August:* Toward a Structuralist Reading." *Modern Language Quarterly* 43 (June 1982):138–55.

Williams, David. *Faulkner's Women: The Myth and the Muse.* Montreal: McGill-Queen's University Press, 1977.

Wittenberg, Judith Bryant. *Faulkner: The Transfiguration of Biography.* Lincoln: University Press of Nebraska Press, 1979.